D1521800

Sowing Change

The Making of Havana's Urban Agriculture

Adriana Premat

Vanderbilt University Press

Nashville

SOWING CHANGE

The Making of Havana's Urban Agriculture

Adriana Premat

Sowing Change

© 2012 by Vanderbilt University Press
Nashville, Tennessee 37235
All rights reserved
First printing 2012

This book is printed on acid-free paper.
Manufactured in the United States of America

Library of Congress Cataloging-in-Publication Data on file
LC control number 2012003435
LC classification S477.C82 H38 2012
Dewey class number 635.9/77

ISBN 978-0-8265-1858-3 (cloth)
ISBN 978-0-8265-1859-0 (paperback)
ISBN 978-0-8265-1860-6 (e-book)

Contents

Preface

I first visited Cuba in 1994, at the peak of the economic crisis that followed the breakup of the Soviet bloc. Then, I was a curious traveler interested in seeing firsthand the socialist nation I had heard so much about as I was growing up in Argentina. As it turned out, particularly in the early 1990s, Cuba was not the place I had imagined. The capital, Havana, was a city in ruins: buildings were falling apart, public transportation was almost nonexistent, and food was a scarce commodity. Yet, amid the despair and disappointment, there were glimmers of hope in the possibility of new projects that promised at least a temporary way out of the crisis. Among them were official collaborations between Cuban institutions and solidarity groups in other countries, which facilitated the efforts of individual Cubans who were already applying their ingenuity to help the country, and themselves, escape the worst effects of the crisis. One area that received special priority in cities was household self-provisioning through the cultivation of vegetable gardens or the raising of animals, from chickens to goats, for food.

During that first visit to Cuba, I had opportunity to witness firsthand many instances of such self-provisioning, but there was one case that proved memorable for me. This involved the New Year's Eve slaughtering of a pig on the balcony of the ninth floor of the highest skyscraper in Havana. The pig had been secretly brought there months prior to ensure the availability of pork for a traditional New Year's feast. The presence of pigs in downtown Havana, while technically illegal, was so common then that Fidel Castro himself had to declare an amnesty on keeping pigs in the city. Although there were other, less controversial expressions of primary food production in the city at the time, it was the memory of this pig that spurred me to return to Cuba in 1997 to begin my now more than decade-long ethnographic inquiry into urban agriculture in Havana. In addition to triggering my interest in primary food production in the city, the paradoxical image of a pig in a modern skyscraper still resonates with me as emblematic of the apparent contradictions contained in the revolutionary government's new policies and programs since the early 1990s. Here was a pig residing in a high-rise building that had been a testament to Cuba's modern aspirations in prerevolutionary times and that now, many decades later, showcased on its ground level one of the first state stores in Havana where Cubans could purchase food in U.S. dollars—the same dollars that a short time earlier had been strictly banned in the country. Here was a pig screaming for its life in the heart of one of the better-off neighborhoods of the capital in a country that not long before had taken great pride in its high-tech, scientific approach to agricultural production. Within a short time, the squealing was over, and a few hours later we were savoring freshly made *chicharrones* (pork cracklings) to welcome the New Year. I was not sure at the time what exactly we were celebrating on that anniversary of the 1959 revolution: our host did not make any political pronouncements and limited himself to commenting on the fine quality of the *chicharrones*.

The 1990s were years of disorienting change for many Cubans. As long-standing state welfare services—including food rations—were severely curtailed across the country and as the peso lost its value, overshadowed by a now freely circulating U.S. dollar, the squealing of pigs, the crowing of roosters, and the bleating of goats, all raised to ensure household food provisions, became increasingly common across Cuban cities. Adding to the disorienting effects that the sounds and smells of these animals provoked in many a city dweller, in places like Havana tourism seemed to be returning Cuba to its infamous prerevolutionary past as lecherous foreign men publicly flaunted their newfound intimacy with much-too-young Cuban women. Further complicating the situation, Cubans who had gone into exile years prior, officially dismissed as unwanted *gusanos* (parasites) by the government, were now returning as welcomed visitors. Laden with dollars and needed goods for their families at a time of great scarcity, these gusanos were rebaptized in Cuban popular parlance as *mariposas* (butterflies)—a term highlighting their desirable metamorphosis. In a country where for decades capitalism had been demonized, foreign capitalists were now publicly invited to join the state in profit-seeking ventures. Although Cuban citizens were repeatedly told that these changes were made to "save socialism," perplexity and outright cynicism appeared to reign among the population. Understandably, against the backdrop of change, many Cubans felt that the conceptual boundaries between city and countryside, modern and "premodern," pre- and post-1959 Cuba, socialism and capitalism, the world within and the world without were coming undone. Whether interpreted as a sign of the imminent downfall of Cuban socialism or as the possibility of its healthy rebirth, these and other crisis-related changes have spawned a lively academic debate about the future of Cuba.

Some of these changes, particularly those connected with urban agriculture, have also received considerable international attention for their relevance beyond the Cuban context. In a world where questions of urban and agricultural sustainability have gained increasing currency, Cuba's urban agriculture experiments, characterized by a drastically reduced reliance on petroleum, a shift toward organic fertilizers and biological pest controls, and shorter distances from field to table, have captured the imagination of those concerned about the rapidly depleting global supplies of petroleum, the ecological footprint of cities, and the detrimental health and environmental effects of industrialized agriculture. For many concerned global citizens, Cuba's recent agricultural challenges foreshadow the possible future of even the most developed countries in the world, holding important lessons for all.

This book engages those interested in Cuba's political future, as well as those who wish to understand the motives, hopes, and struggles of Cubans engaged in urban agriculture today, by providing a unique perspective on these topics that is grounded in place and in the process of place making. Specifically, the book considers the places where pigs, like the one I saw in 1994, continue to be raised, alongside rabbits, chickens, and guinea pigs; places where plantains, avocados, cassava, and peppers are grown in small gardens tended by a mostly aging population who, while contributing to the international fame of Cuba's urban agriculture movement, remain largely anonymous and poorly understood. It is the contention of this book that these places can provide important insights into the dynamics of sustainable development, transnational governance, and state power in contemporary Cuba.

As an anthropologist trained to suspect the perspective "from above," I first approached these places from the vantage point of those who live closest to the ground: the urban farmers themselves. However, I soon realized that to adequately understand the creation and transformation of these primary food production sites, I needed to look beyond the producers to other actors, variously situated in Havana's urban agriculture field—from high-level government officials to employees at internationally funded Cuban nongovernmental organizations (NGOs).

In a country where people have previously been taught to be cautious when talking to foreigners, I found that most individuals, regardless of their social location, were remarkably willing to share their knowledge and experience of urban agriculture with me. Given my Latin American background, I was often welcomed as a member of an "imagined community" that shared not only a common language and a similar history but also some of the same revolutionary icons (I was often reminded that I came from the birthplace of Ernesto "Che" Guevara, the fondly remembered "adopted son" of the Cuban revolution).

As I picked up Cuban speech idioms, my skin darkened with the sun, and people noted my repeated trips and willingness to experience the life of ordinary citizens, I was often introduced to others with flattering phrases such as "*Es casi cubana*" (she's nearly Cuban) or "*está aplatanada*" (literally, she has become plantain-like, meaning totally adapted to the place). Yet I knew these were compliments often applied even to those having rudimentary knowledge of the language and the place. I was very aware throughout my research that, unlike Che, I never attained "native" status and could not erase my special position as a foreigner (a difference marked, among other things, by my relative wealth vis-à-vis the people with whom I worked and my ability to freely travel across national boundaries).

The advantages afforded by my special status were highlighted during an interview I conducted with a man who raised rabbits on his home patio. When I hesitated in formulating a question, he interrupted me, saying, "Go ahead, ask me anything you want and I will respond honestly because, technically, I will not hide anything from you because you are not from here." These views were echoed by other urban agriculture practitioners who, given my outsider status, came to consider me a safe confidant on a range of topics—including personal family problems, illicit activities, and critiques of the status quo within the urban agriculture field and beyond.

While my special status as an outsider sometimes earned me people's trust, it also made me and my research suspect, in certain situations. This was made patently clear to me on one occasion when, after having been invited to attend an urban-agriculture-related meeting at the Communist Party Cadre School in the outskirts of Havana, I was politely told by a lower-ranking Ministry of Agriculture official to step out for the rest of the meeting because somebody had questioned a foreigner being in attendance. I complied and sat out in the sun until the meeting was over. Afterward, the higher-ranking officials, who had invited me in the first place, seemed embarrassed by this situation but could not quite explain it. By all accounts, nothing new had transpired at the meeting, except that the minister of agriculture had confirmed that small-scale producers could now sell their produce from their homes. Later, a friend who attended the meeting commented that this incident illustrated the generalized paranoia toward foreigners that still reigns in certain formal settings.

From the time I first started conducting research in Havana, in 1997, I had experienced this suspicion only one other time. I had formally requested an interview with the provincial president of the Urban Agriculture Department in Havana and was subsequently invited to go to the office headquarters. What I did not realize at first was that department officials were going to interview me, to satisfy their curiosity about what I was doing in Cuba. Though unexpected, the experience did not upset me. After all, I felt and continue to feel that Cubans—regardless of their position concerning my research—have every right to ask these questions of me and other foreign researchers doing work there. By then, I had already come into contact with other foreign researchers and knew that not all of them were ethical in their research practices, sometimes being intentionally deceptive and determined to prove their ideologically driven a priori conclusions about the "Cuban regime."

I was eventually invited back for other meetings at the Party Cadre School and was granted an interview with the very person from the Urban Agriculture Department in Havana who had first interviewed me about my research. In addition to my daily involvement in the lives of the urban farmers I chose to work with, I was regularly invited to participate in meetings, workshops, and classes related to urban agriculture, and I seldom turned down such invitations, whether they came from institutions or from farmers with whom I had become friends. While, for the most part, the interactions I had with middle- and high-ranking officials within the urban agriculture field did not move them to speak outside the realm of what I came to recognize as the officially sanctioned discourse on urban agriculture, I saw no reason to dismiss their perspectives since they only enriched my knowledge of the phenomenon I was trying to understand.

In the first two chapters of the book I explore how state actors with official authority to name and regulate space within Cuba conceive and represent urban agriculture and its related locales. Chapter 1 outlines how, as a result of changing material conditions in post-1989 Cuba, pertinent state actors had to reconsider established patterns of urban land use, agricultural production, food provisioning, and governance in order to make room for urban agriculture. Chapter 2 shows how urban agriculture sites have been discursively constituted as emblems of revolutionary struggle, while at the same time being suspected of fostering unwanted deviations from desirable socialist conduct.

In the next couple of chapters, leaving behind official state representations and practices, I consider the lived experience of those who inhabit the small-scale urban agriculture sites where I conducted the bulk of my research. Chapter 3 demonstrates how involvement in these sites reflects producers' marginalization from the most dynamic sectors of the Cuban economy and from projects currently prioritized by the government. The chapter further illustrates how, even in the case of public land, producers manage to carve out a space of their own that ultimately reflects their needs and desires as pertains to food security and overall physical and emotional health. Chapter 4 reveals how successful production in these small-scale, self-provisioning sites leads to critical reflection on current and prior state practices pertaining to food security, the organization of agricultural space, urban planning, and vertical models of authority and knowledge.

The two subsequent chapters illustrate how small-scale, self-provisioning urban agriculture sites are created and re-created in response to changing personal and national projects, which in turn are influenced by a range of international actors that, in one way or another, connect with needed material resources. Specifically, Chapter 5 focuses on a site located on public land, while Chapter 6 follows the trajectory of another located on private property. The chapters trace the transformation of these sites as they are incorporated into projects that aspire to model ideals of community contribution and environmental responsibility. As the analysis explores issues related to agency, self-discipline, material limitations, and the power derived from ultimate control over space and other resources, the line between voluntary action and imposition "from above" (whether guided by the state hierarchy or by international funders working through Cuban NGOs) becomes blurred, revealing a complex landscape of power.

Chapter 7 discusses how urban agriculture sites are materially constituted out of global connections and exchanges that bring together personal, national, and international projects. It further shows how Havana's urban agriculture sites become symbols of alternative development on the global stage that in turn affect the development of these sites at home.

The conclusion summarizes the insights derived from the research, highlighting how urban agriculture and, in particular, the small-scale sites that constitute the primary focus of the book constitute fertile grounds for exploring shifting power landscapes in Cuba and the ongoing reconfiguration of the socialist project.

Acknowledgments

As with all research projects that span over a decade, this one has benefited from the support of many individuals and institutions. Among the latter, I want to mention the financial support received from the Social Sciences Research Council of Canada, the Agropolis Program at the International Development Research Centre, and the University of Western Ontario. I also want to thank everyone at Vanderbilt University Press, especially my acquisitions editor, Eli Bortz, for having committed to this book.

Among those in Cuba, I want to acknowledge, first and foremost, the urban farmers who shared their lives and perspectives with me since, without them, there would be no book. During my repeated visits to Cuba, I became friends with many of them but also met many others who, while not agriculturally inclined, nevertheless helped this project through their hospitality and with their insights as Havana residents. Here, I want to make special mention of my most loyal friends on the island, Hector and Reynaldo, who, in the early years of my fieldwork, willfully worked themselves into my research by signing up for a permaculture course and even getting a pig of their own, which they baptized Adriana in my honor! The entire permaculture team at the Fundación Antonio Núñez Jiménez de la Naturaleza y el Hombre (FANJNH) was most helpful to me over the years, taking me on garden tours, introducing me to urban farmers and institutional actors, and even registering me in a number of their sustainable agriculture courses, one of which I barely passed with my friend Hector. Among the FANJNH staff, I am most grateful to the woman I call Luisa in the text, who went well beyond her institutional obligations by sharing with me her excitement over various garden projects and her most precious contacts in the field. I also want to express my indebtedness to the many urban agriculture professionals from the Ministry of Agriculture and other institutions mentioned in the text who guided my work and often corrected my misconceptions about the field.

Among those outside Cuba, I want to acknowledge my professors at York University in Toronto, Canada, in particular my MA supervisor, Malcolm Blincow; my PhD supervisor, Margaret Rodman; and my graduate adviser, Penny Van Esterik, for the guidance they provided me as I matured as a researcher and an anthropologist. As I initiated the process of writing this book I received valuable feedback from Jean-François Millaire, my current colleague at the University of Western Ontario, and his wife, Magali Morlion. Their enthusiasm and encouragement, as well as the gentle prodding and moral support given to me by my colleagues Randa Farah and Kim Clark, made all the difference in the summer of 2010, when I really thought this book project would never get off the ground.

As I neared the final phases of preparing the manuscript for publication, there were many others who lent a helping hand. I want to express appreciation to my student, Aaron Lawrence, for his proofreading skills and, last but not least, to the two external anonymous reviewers, who, through their thoughtful feedback, made me aware of important gaps in the data I had initially presented.

Although through the years that span this book there have been many loved ones who have lent me their support and a fresh pair of eyes, when needed, I want to especially express my gratitude to Robin Turnbull and Sean Brotherton, who, for over a decade, have sustained me, intellectually and emotionally, with their friendship and almost daily phone conversations. With Sean in particular, I have been fortunate to share not just the York graduate experience but also the challenges and pleasures of doing research in Cuba, from unpleasant encounters with overzealous institutional gatekeepers to good conversation, food, laughter, and mojitos.

In addition to friends and colleagues, I want to thank my family for being supportive of my work and because they are all, in part, responsible for the sensibilities that have guided my writing. If there's any good storytelling in this book, it is due to the teachings of my mother. As for the rigor of my argument, I know that it has been greatly improved by the input of my father, who has always been the most relentless of critics and the most reliable of editors. Finally, I want to acknowledge the inspiration given to me by my partner, David, who has taught me that you can never go too wrong when you let an honest heartbeat permeate your writing.

Needless to say, any failings in this text are my own. I can only hope that those who participated in this project, many of whom for various reasons could not be mentioned in these acknowledgments, are able to see their teachings and their perspectives partly reflected in the following pages.

Introduction

A New Global Sense of Place
and Rooted Landscapes

After the dissolution of the Soviet bloc, beginning in 1989, Cuba had to shift, as Susan Eckstein (1994) aptly put it, from a position of "communist solidarity" to one of "communist solitary," being "forced" by the sudden deterritorialization of its strongest world allies to re-create its links with nonsocialist countries and international investors. As Cuba refashioned itself out of new global connections and disconnections, life on the island was considerably transformed.[1] Recent academic publications on the country have variously explored the impact of the government's selective openings to the world, as well as the strategies deployed by some of its residents to activate or reactivate their own worldly connections.[2] Some authors have illustrated how such unevenly distributed openings and connections have significantly altered residents' sense of place, their sense of self, and their relationship to *la revolución*,[3] its leadership, and the socialist state.[4]

This book expands on this literature by charting the transnational flows that have since contributed to the production of those rooted landscapes associated with urban agriculture in Havana from a perspective that does not lose sight of the particular emplacement of the "global" in the national and local contexts.[5] In this respect, and as is fitting for a book that focuses on an activity like agriculture that demands of practitioners a grounded knowledge (and that, as will be seen, is carried out by people who are remarkably fixed in space), the analysis pays particular attention to place itself, focusing on the symbolic and material production of some of the places where urban agriculture has taken root.

Guided by Henri Lefebvre's (1998 [1974]) seminal work on the social production of space, the book follows the development of urban agriculture sites, simultaneously considering their material and lived dimensions, as well as the official representations and practices associated with them in the public realm. Insofar as Havana's urban agriculture sites are dynamic, contested, and ever-changing products of multiple agents with differing authority over space and needed resources, paying careful attention to the processes involved in their production inevitably leads to an exploration of power dynamics in this socialist nation.

Through my research, I knew that the cultivation of vegetables and the raising of food animals were not new activities in Havana. Since 1959, the revolutionary government had, at different times, endorsed primary food production in the city, whether to deal with periods of food scarcity or to support ambitious plans for the agricultural development of the urban periphery (Dumont 1970; Scarpaci, Coyula, and Segre 1997). Government campaigns aside, of course, there had always been people in Havana who had engaged in small-scale agricultural production, whether to supplement government rations or continue with family traditions (Butterworth 1980; Cruz Hernández and Murciano 1996). What was different about the early 1990s was not just the sudden, spontaneous en masse surge in primary food production in the city but the extent to which governmental and nongovernmental, domestic and foreign institutions mobilized to support the activity.

The sites my research focused on not only were officially encouraged and assisted by a range of state actors, from urban planners to Ministry of Agriculture officials, but also were guided and assisted by domestic NGO staff as well as international garden activists, development agencies, and NGOs based in capitalist countries. Further complicating this picture, independent citizens who engaged in urban agriculture, through their own creativity and spontaneous acts, also transformed the way the activity was conceived and practiced in the city. With this taken into account, the challenge in writing this book has been to find a way to convey the complex and dynamic historical processes involved in the making of urban agriculture sites in Havana without falling into the trap of unfairly emphasizing only one dimension, set of actors, or set of pertinent factors.

Drawing in part on Michel Foucault's (1979, 1991) writings on disciplinary technologies and governmentality, I consider how the discursive practices of governmental and nongovernmental institutional actors, both domestic and international, have guided the actions and thoughts of Havana's urban farmers in ways that have influenced the evolution of urban agriculture sites.

Inspired by the ideas of Michel de Certeau (1988), who drew attention to the creative and subversive everyday practices of those who inhabit spaces that are named, tabulated, and regulated by others, I explore how urban farmers contradict, unsettle, redefine, and complicate the designs and practices of government officials and NGO players working for domestic or international organizations. Applying Certeau's (1988, xxii) questions to the topic of urban agriculture in Havana, I ask, how do urban farmers "insinuate their countless differences into the dominant text," and how do their private, unpublicized, and underground practices reveal the ambiguities and gaps of the master plan executed by those who are presumed to be in charge?

Finally, I strive to give adequate attention to the material dimension of urban agriculture sites. I carefully consider the physical aspects of the primary food production sites used in my analysis, noting transformations in layout, design, and infrastructure, and tracing, whenever possible, how these transformations connect to individual desires or pressures from institutional actors. Still dealing with the material dimension of the sites, I also follow the flow of needed resources from national institutions or international funders, showing how the practices of all Cubans involved are influenced by material conditions and considerations—although they can never be reduced to such factors alone.

For this account, I draw on ethnographic data collected from 1997 to 2009. The bulk of the analysis relies on research conducted in those small-scale self-provisioning urban agriculture sites known in the urban agriculture field as *parcelas* and *patios* (see Table 1).[6] These sites are located on usufruct land and privately owned spaces, respectively. The

3

usufruct lots encompass places that had previously been demolition sites, playing fields, and even portions of public parks. The private spaces, on the other hand, include home patios, alleyways, and rooftops. Geared mainly toward family self-provisioning, both types of sites, which by 2002 were said to number approximately a hundred thousand in Havana alone (Companioni et al. 2002), are officially recognized as distinct from other categories of agricultural sites in the city (see Table 1). What drew me to focus on them, in addition to ease of access, was their grounding in the domestic sphere and their distinctive connections to transnational capital flows, international assistance, and national and international imaginaries.

Given their perceived distance from the state, parcelas and patios were, from the onset of the post-1989 economic crisis, spaces of choice for international funders who desired to assist the population without working directly with the Cuban socialist state. Over time, and despite

Table 1. Main food-oriented urban agricultural sites in Havana as per Cruz Hernández and Sánchez Medina's description (2001)

Production Sites	Land Tenure	Area Occupied	Main Objective
Fincas (farms)	private/ state	N/A	Commercialization
Organopónicos Populares (popular organoponic)	state	2000–5000 sq. meters	Commercialization
Huertos intensivos (intensive gardens)	state	1000–3000 sq. meters	Commercialization
Organopónicos de Alto Rendimiento (OAR) (high yield organoponic)	state	> 1 hectare	Commercialization
Autoconsumo estatal (factory/enterprise self-provisioning gardens)	state	> 1 hectare	Provisioning of work-place dining rooms
Parcela (usufruct plots)	state	<1000 sq. meters	Household self-provisioning
"Productive" Patio	private	<1000 sq. meters	Household self-provisioning

considerable changes in Havana's urban agriculture field, these sites have retained their privileged position in the funding schemes of many domestic and international NGOs. Importantly, parcelas and patios have continued to capture the imagination of activists all over the world interested in alternative development models and, in particular, in the pursuit of sustainable agriculture and healthier urban environments.

Within Havana's official urban agriculture movement, parcelas and patios also occupy a special place. In the early 1990s, at a time when the state had few resources to dedicate to the creation of larger sites like the *organopónicos de alto rendimiento* (high-yield organoponic gardens), it was these small-scale self-provisioning spaces that became the inspiring face of Havana's urban agriculture movement.[7] The patios, then usually referred to as *huertos particulares, familiares,* or *caseros* (private, family, or home gardens), were regularly celebrated in the media (Chong 1991; Pages 1991), while the parcelas, then known as *huertos populares, comunitarios,* or *colectivos* (popular, communitarian, or collective gardens), received even more attention given their public status. According to one of the founders of the city's Urban Agriculture Department, these sites played a key symbolic role in creating "the powerful image of a city producing food on every corner," symbolizing Cuba's struggle for survival.[8] Indeed, week after week, city newspapers reported on the ways in which these agricultural spaces spread across Havana with headlines such as "Gardens Advance with Giant Steps," "Popular Gardens Grow," "Popular Cultivation: A Growing Field," "The Cultivation of Vacant Lots Advances," "Sixty Percent of Vacant Lots Sown as Popular Gardens," and "Sowing Willpower: A Capital City of Vegetable Gardens."[9]

Beginning in 1994, parcelas and patios gradually lost the spotlight of the media to the organopónicos, which, being larger in scale, appeared to offer a better solution for the food security needs of a broader sector of the population.[10] Yet, unlike organopónicos, which among other things required the regular importation of massive amounts of soil from other ecosystems, parcelas and patios represented a more sustainable form of production, one that could arguably better assist in "greening" the city while contributing to healthier social and physical environments. For these and other reasons, by 2000, patios and parcelas had become the focus of a state-led movement that recognized not just their food-security contributions, for which they had been aptly celebrated in the past, but also their potential in helping create healthier social and physical urban environments.

Although, over the years, I visited many parcelas and patios in Havana, in my research I primarily focused on twenty-nine of these sites associated with forty-two producers, twenty-nine men and thirteen women, mostly over the age of fifty-five.[11] I also worked with twenty-one female and twenty male representatives of twenty-seven pertinent official bodies, including state agencies and NGOs, whose jurisdictions ranged from the local to the national level. Included were the Ministry of Agriculture (MINAG), the Institute for Fundamental Research on Tropical Agriculture (INIFAT), the Agricultural Input Enterprise (ESA), the Agricultural Consultation and Input Stores, the Committees for the Defense of the Revolution (CDRs), the Cuban Association for Animal Production (ACPA), the Revolutionary Armed Forces (FAR), the Provincial Urban Planning and Architecture Office (DPPFA), the Group for the Holistic Development of the Capital (GDIC), the Antonio Núñez Jiménez Foundation for Nature and Humanity (FANJNH), the Cuban Council of Churches, the Office of the Historian of the City, and the Juan Tomás Roig Cuban Botanical Association. The analysis was further informed by formal and informal conversations, while in Cuba, with foreign staff from a range of international development agencies and non-Cuban NGOs, including UN-HABITAT Cuba, the Australian Conservation Foundation, and, from Canada, the Evergreen Foundation and LifeCycles.

As well as relying on the knowledge gained through participant observation, interviews, and informal discussions with both urban farmers and institutional actors, this book also draws on archival and library research conducted at the Cuban National Library, the Center for the Americas Library, the MINAG Library, the GDIC's Information Center, and the Special Collections Library at the FANJNH.

I tried my best to incorporate the differing voices and perspectives of everyone I worked with, allowing their fragmented and sometimes contradictory nature to come through. I made no attempt to iron out inconsistencies but rather chose to contextualize them as best I could. To this end, whenever possible, I provided personal information about the individuals being discussed, as well as information about the context in which certain statements were pronounced or actions carried out.[12]

My resulting reflections on the production of urban agriculture sites in Havana led me to an analysis that centers, to a large extent, on the underpinnings of Cuban state power—a topic I had hoped to downplay since it seemed to me that the Cuban state had become an unhealthy obsession in much of the academic and nonacademic literature on post-1959 Cuba. Much as anthropologists of India seemed unable to separate India, the place, from the concept of hierarchy (Appadurai 1988b), foreign researchers working in Cuba, as pointed out by Antoni Kapcia (2008), do not seem to be able to think of Cuba beyond the state (sometimes collapsed into the figure of Fidel Castro, whether as benevolent or malevolent dictator). Thus, when my reflections on the production of urban agriculture sites unexpectedly led me to reflect on the power of the Cuban state, I feared that I, too, was falling victim to what Appadurai (1988a) described as anthropologists' predilection for "localizing ideas." Yet my reflections on the Cuban state, from the perspective of urban agriculture and its associated sites, seemed to lead to a fruitful questioning of common understandings of the bases and the limits of state power in that country.

From Urban Agriculture to the Limits of State Power

By 1997, the year I began my research in Havana, urban agriculture appeared to occupy a relatively marginal position within Cuban development schemes. Falling mostly within the "peso sector" of the economy when the dollar or hard currency sector was becoming increasingly important, urban agriculture seemed distant from the most dynamic axis of societal transformation.[13] In this sense, the activity presented itself as a poor candidate to measure the pulse of what most political analysts considered a portentous time of change in Cuba. Yet in other ways, urban agriculture was emblematic of the times, reflecting major societal transformations initiated in the country over the past decades.

Urban agriculture reflected the rapid movement toward decentralization set off in Cuba as a result of the breakup of the Soviet bloc.[14] With shrinking resources at its command, the Cuban government found itself unable to guarantee basic necessities for the population at large and had to shift many of its previous service-provisioning functions to the nonstate sector. This involved, among other things, the encouragement of private agricultural production geared to commercialization, as well as the promotion of the kind of family self-provisioning associated with parcelas and patios. The latter, as mentioned earlier, were partially supported by domestic and foreign NGOs that were allowed to fill the void left by the state's lack of material resources.

Inasmuch as urban agriculture represented the partial transfer of responsibilities in the area of food security from the state to individual citizens and nonstate institutions, it illustrated the withdrawal of the state from a domain pregnant with political connotations. Over the years, the Cuban state had established its role as primary provider of basic necessities, such as food, and it was in this area that the efficacy (and legitimacy) of the socialist system was put to its toughest test. As a Cuban writer humorously put it, "The world's sages sent an economic specialist here one day, and people told him that the Cuban revolution had only three problems: breakfast, lunch, and dinner" (quoted in North American Congress on Latin America 1995, 27). In this context, the incursion of foreign funding—originating in capitalist countries and channeled through Cuban NGOs—in support of independent, small-scale urban farmers in places like Havana could be expected to undermine the power of the state and its associated political project. Indeed, since the early years of the Cuban economic crisis, some analysts in and outside Cuba have forecasted that this type of foreign assistance could result in the weakening of state power and the eventual downfall of Cuban socialism. This book queries such predictions by investigating the extent to which the Cuban state at this time became but one node among others in a shifting landscape of power that opened up a space for nonstate visions and projects to flourish.[15] It further asks whether or not these nonstate visions and projects actually worked against the grain of Cuban socialism.

The transfer of responsibilities to the nonstate sector was arguably accompanied by an important shift in the practice of governance as individual citizens became responsible for ensuring their own well-being and, to a certain extent, gained the right to make their own choices in the area of subsistence. Although most urban agriculture sites in Havana retained links with state institutions, the sites my research focused on—namely, the parcelas and patios—were characterized by considerable autonomy from the state control apparatus. As will be seen, in a context where the state had lost its prior capacity to allocate resources and enforce compliance with established regulations, these small-scale urban agriculture sites could, but did not always, constitute a threat to state power. In this respect, these sites offered an opportunity to explore both the weaknesses and strengths of the public apparatus of government, which Antonio Gramsci (1971) called "political society." They further provided a chance to investigate how state power, in Cuba as elsewhere, is not just reinforced through coercive mechanisms and government institutions but also embedded in civil society and the everyday practices voluntarily carried out by "average" citizens without the need for direct involvement, or forceful pressure, from state actors.

Starting from ethnographic material that primarily focuses on Havana's parcelas and patios, this book, then, not only traces the evolution of this city's urban agriculture movement but also, importantly, explores the limits and resilience of the Cuban state at a particular historical juncture when new social actors, as well as contradictory government projects, seemed to be redefining and even undermining policies and priorities long associated with Cuban socialism.

Figure 1.1. A typical organopónico in the city of Havana.

1

Shifting Socialist Spatial Dreams

Institutional Visions and Revisions

At the corner of Forty-Fourth Street and Fifth Avenue—one of the widest avenues in the city—in the municipality of Playa, in the district of Miramar, amid embassies and old mansions inhabited by diplomats, Cuban celebrities, and high government functionaries, one finds an *organopónico*: a large lot of approximately one hectare with rows of raised container beds used for growing a wide array of vegetables and herbs, including lettuce, spinach, and radishes (see Figure 1.1). This was the first garden of its type in Havana. It was named INRE after the National Institute of State Reserves, from which came the person responsible for the garden's creation: Brigadier General Moisés Sio Wong.[1] A veteran of the 1959 revolutionary struggle, Sio Wong grew up in Havana. As if to underscore the agricultural potential of the area, he told me he still remembered how, in prerevolutionary times, U.S. ferries frequently docked in the city harbor to pick up tomatoes grown in Cuba. Being of Chinese background, he had especially fond memories of the vegetable gardens, then located in various parts of the city, tended by Chinese horticulturalists who peddled their produce door-to-door. These gardens, which were remembered fondly by other Havana residents of the same generation, disappeared after the revolution as the city modernized, and this kind of private production and sale of fresh produce was halted in favor of a state-run food distribution system.[2]

As a young revolutionary, General Sio Wong had envisioned momentous transformations for his country and had enthusiastically participated in the "revolutionary process" that had aimed to turn Cuba into a modern socialist nation. At that time, he could never have imagined finding himself, at the turn of the millennium, talking to curious foreigners like me, in his office at the National Institute of State Reserves, about farming without tractors or chemical inputs in one of the poshest areas of Havana, on a site that was not naturally suited for agricultural production. Then again, these were exceptional times that called for the implementation of extraordinary ideas if the government was to retain its commitment to ensuring national food security.

After reviewing the priority given to food security in socialist Cuba, this chapter outlines the manner in which the government, in an attempt to deal with an unprecedented food crisis, made room for urban agriculture in post-1989 Havana. Specifically, the chapter considers how this effort was accompanied by a reconceptualization of agricultural production, urban land use, and the ultimate role of the state in the development of the nation. Previously, the modus operandi in sectors like agriculture and urban planning fit a pattern James Scott (1998) attributes to "authoritarian, high-modernist states," which privilege state-centralized, large-scale projects that rest on global abstractions and blind confidence in scientific and technological progress. In the field of agriculture, as will be seen, the Cuban government had taken pride in having a highly industrialized, large-scale sector reliant on the latest chemical inputs and other scientific innovations. When it came to city planning and renovation schemes, the emphasis had been on the rational allocation of services and resources through centralized planning that excluded primary food production from the urban core.

In this context, the shift to urban agriculture represented a radical break that, from the perspectives of state actors outlined in this chapter, exemplified the kinds of adaptations, tensions, and negotiations that have characterized the Special Period in Times of Peace (hereafter Special Period)—a phrase introduced by the Cuban government to refer to the series of economic adjustments and related deprivations brought about by the acute economic crisis that followed the breakup of the Soviet bloc. This exposition reveals how those having official authority to regulate and design space do not represent a single, univocal perspective, as authors like Certeau (1988) presume, but rather reflect multivocal and ambiguous projects that allow for contestation and revision "from below" as well as from within established authority circles—a point that is particularly important to make when it comes to a place like Cuba, whose state apparatus is often caricatured as monolithic, homogeneous, and unchanging.

Ultimately, the analysis presented here and in the following chapter illustrates a vigorous struggle under way within and across Cuban state institutions as the country was "forced" to move away from previously hegemonic conceptualizations of space, and from forms of food production and distribution that advocated rational, large-scale planning and full integration into the formal state apparatus as the only way to ensure the well-being of the majority and the subsequent health of *la revolución*.

The Struggle for Universal Food Security in Socialist Cuba

In his famous self-defense speech during the court proceedings against him after he led the failed attack on the Moncada Barracks on July 26, 1957 (meant to be the opening salvo in a struggle to overthrow the reigning Batista dictatorship), a young Fidel Castro (1993, 65) stated that "it is inconceivable that people should go to sleep hungry when there is still land [in Cuba] left to be cultivated." In 1959, when the leaders of the 26th of July revolutionary movement (named after that failed first attempt) finally came to power, the attainment of national food security was central to the new government's agenda. Over the years, this concern was reflected, in part, in government policies that changed the tenure status of agricultural land as well as the organizational forms of agricultural production so that, in effect, the state obtained almost total control of official agricultural production and distribution.

The portion of state land used for production of food destined for national consumption shifted as Cuba's international political and economic alliances changed. Beginning in 1972, for example, a trade agreement with the Soviet Union led the Cuban government to emphasize production of sugar and citrus fruits to be exchanged for cereals and

13

other food products from Soviet bloc countries (Burchardt 2000, 172). While some analysts note that this trading arrangement allowed the Cuban government to "provide a greater quantity and variety of food-stuffs to its population" (Rosset and Benjamin 1994, 12), it also encouraged a dangerous dedication to the production of single-export crops, like sugar, and a reliance on food imports. By the late 1980s, only 40 percent of cultivable land was dedicated to the production of nonexport food crops (Burchardt 2000, 172). Despite intense efforts in the early 1960s and the late 1980s to achieve self-sufficiency in foodstuffs, import dependency remained high. In the early 1990s, 55 percent of the calories, 50 percent of the proteins, and 90 percent of the fats consumed in Cuba were imported (Burchardt 2000, 173).

The attainment of national food security, however, remained explicitly central to the government's project. This project involved more than state management of most agricultural land and production; it included the equitable distribution of basic food products, national or imported, at affordable prices. While the Cuban government did for decades succeed in eradicating hunger, scarcity of certain food products was a chronic problem in postrevolutionary times. This problem was addressed, in part, by the creation of a rationing system. Regardless of its various flaws (Dumont 1970, 80–81; Benjamin, Collins, and Scott 1986), the ration, instituted on March 12, 1962, more than any other Cuban institution instilled in citizens the notion of national food equity while re-creating the state as its guarantor (Premat 1998; Díaz Vázquez 2000, 55).[3]

Except for a brief period of experimentation with the Free Farmers Market in the 1980s, for decades the state remained the primary food provider: it was in charge of ration stores and other official venues where food was sold and also managed the allocation of food to schools and workplaces. In this context, the power of the state was at least partly based on its near monopoly over food, both its production and its distribution. Yet this monopoly was also its Achilles' heel. This would become particularly evident after the breakup of the Soviet bloc, when Cuba faced one of its worse food crisis since 1959—a crisis that, according to some, necessitated entirely new mind-sets.

Cultivating New Ideas: Making a Stronger Revolution

In the fall of 2001, the First Annual National Meeting of the Patio and Parcela Movement convened at the Provincial School for Communist Party Cadres in an outlying district of Havana. Seated at a long table, presiding over the meeting, were General Sio Wong, representing INRE; Alberto Jordán, the minister of agriculture; Adolfo Nodals, the national president of the Urban Agriculture Department; and Juan Contino Aslan, the national president of the CDRs—the mass organizations that, since 1960, have rallied neighborhood support for state-endorsed political, health, and educational campaigns. During one of his many interventions at the meeting, Contino commented on how important it was for Havana families to grow vegetables and fruit trees in their homes, saying, "We are cultivating the revolutionary project; this is an ideological job because we refuse to create a society of consumers! We refuse to have the capital city fed by the rest of the country."

For those in the audience, the majority of whom were young adults in the early years of the revolution, Contino's words must have triggered memories of the mass mobilizations of the 1960s, when large-scale *granjas del pueblo* (people's farms) were created and urbanites were sent to the countryside to learn to produce the food they had learned to consume so well in the city. A typical article of the time in the magazine *Bohemia* eulogized the involvement of city dwellers in agricultural labor, arguing that such activity would help undermine "bureaucracy, the weed of public life that threatens the triumphs of the revolution," adding that this was "sacrifice of adipose tissue, of superfluous fat, in favor of the nerve and the muscle" that would help build "the New Cuba" (anonymous 1967).

The talk of creating a better Cuba and a stronger revolution through engagement in the cultivation of the land was still current in 2001, but, as Contino's other pronouncements illustrated, the way in which this engagement was framed had changed considerably. Contino elaborated: "Today, we talk about a battle of ideas, we talk about sowing ideas, and I believe that sowing the notion that the patio of one's home can be an edible garden is very important. . . . We are planting trees, sowing vegetables, creating food, but at the same time we are sowing ideas to make an ever more resilient Revolution." Among other things, these new ideas involved a reconceptualization of agricultural activity that left behind the national scale of the people's farms in favor of edible gardens in private home patios that could supplement the family's diet and contribute to the creation of "greener" urban environments.

Since the commencement of the Special Period, making a "more resilient revolution" meant, among other things, "sowing new ideas" regarding which policies and practices were acceptable in the pursuit of national well-being. Hence, development paths previously dismissed as antithetical to revolutionary goals, such as the promotion of large-scale international tourism, foreign investment in revenue-generating enterprises, and low-input, small-scale forms of agricultural production, would be explored. During our conversation in February 2001, General Sio Wong told me: "[These] are measures we had to take to save socialism. We still do not like some of them but we had to prioritize survival."

Rethinking Food Production and the Place of Agriculture

Scaling Down Agricultural Dreams

The Ministry of Agriculture (MINAG) and, in special cases, the Revolutionary Armed Forces (Fuerzas Armadas Revolucionarias, FAR) had for years been in charge of monitoring, regulating, and encouraging agricultural development in revolutionary Cuba. From the perspectives of these state institutions and of the revolutionary leadership, agriculture belonged in rural areas or the outskirts of cities, with the optimum organization and use of agricultural space taking the form of large tracts of land worked with modern technologies thought to ensure the greatest production outputs.

The dissolution of favorable trade relations with the Soviet bloc in the late 1980s forced a difficult "paradigm shift" in these Cuban agricultural visions as the country had to shift from a high-tech, high-input approach reliant on imports to a scaled-down, "green" approach associated with self-reliant, sustainable, organic agricultural practices. In January 2001, León Vega, the director of international relations at the MINAG, illustrated the extent of "new thinking" and adaptation involved as he told me about the new schools for ox drivers. Prior to 1989, the ratio of tractors in use to population in Cuba was 1:146—triple that of the United States for the same period (Rosset and Benjamin 1994, 10). Now, Vega commented, "We have trained 200,000 oxen [in an attempt to adapt to reduced gasoline imports]. I think we must be the only country nowadays that has a school for ox drivers. We used to have 90,000 tractors in the country. . . . We had to abandon that path." He further elaborated,

> From the socialist bloc we would buy a million tons of fertilizers; two million tons of animal feed; 30,000 tons of pesticides a year; all the tractors that were needed; and the most important thing: oil. All of this was to disappear in a year and half. . . . In 1989, we used to expend 274 kilograms of fertilizer for a ton of output; now we obtain the same with 29 kilograms. We used to produce a ton with 4.2 kilograms of pesticides and now we do it with 1.1 with the help of biological products, combined with holistic pest management.

Such examples vividly underscore the nature and scale of the technological shifts described by foreign specialists as "the largest conversion from conventional agriculture to organic or semi-organic farming that the world has ever known" (Rosset and Benjamin 1994, 5).

These technological shifts were accompanied by a literal scaling down of agricultural space as small-scale production units became the most efficient way to organize the food production sector at this time. General Sio Wong commented on the initial resistance encountered toward this downsizing of agriculture in a country where, for years, an emphasis on large-scale projects had been the norm: "[This] was small-scale production, about which there were many mental blocks. The idea being that it could not solve the larger alimentary problems."

Still, as imports of food, oil, fertilizers, animal feed, and pesticides from the Soviet Union plummeted, the Cuban government found itself both unable to produce sufficient food on its large state farms and unable to efficiently distribute to the cities what food was produced by the state or independent growers. Under these circumstances, decentralizing agriculture and encouraging food production in cities became a governmental necessity.

Decentralizing Food Production
and Bringing Agriculture to the Barrio

When it came to agricultural land tenure and production, the first thirty years of pertinent revolutionary policy were encapsulated in the slogan "more state property, more socialism" (Burchardt 2000, 171). By the late 1980s, after two agrarian reforms and a series of policies aimed at centralizing agricultural production, 80 percent of Cuba's agricultural land was either owned or managed by the state.[4] For decades, the revolutionary leadership appeared convinced that larger territorial units and rational, centralized state management would lead to higher agricultural production. The individual farmer independently working a small plot with low levels of technology was perceived as "the most backward form of production"; cooperatives were ranked second best, and the large state farms known as granjas del pueblo—owned by "the people" and worked by salaried workers with modern technologies—were considered the "superior" form of production (Benjamin, Collins, and Scott 1986, 167). This emphasis on large-scale and state-run forms of agricultural production had already come under attack in political circles prior to the economic crisis. Still, suggested alternatives for organizing agriculture gained force only when crisis-related shortages necessitated a radical shift.

In September 1993, Law 142, which allowed for the fragmentation of state farms and state agricultural enterprises, initiated the still ongoing move toward the decentralization of food production. This 1993 statute began what was unofficially baptized the Third Agrarian Reform, which involved the transfer—through usufruct rights—of 70 percent of Cuba's agricultural land, previously under state ownership and management, to independent individuals or to producers organized in peasant associations and cooperatives (Burchardt 2000). Sometimes this involved giving land back to the same families of producers who had in previous years leased their land to the government for use in large-scale production programs. As one urban planner described it, in the case of the green belt around Havana, this reversed the efforts carried out in the late 1960s, when the fences that characterized farmland in the area had come down to give way to the boundless landscape of the granjas del pueblo.[5]

Although it was not directly the result of laws intended for application to traditional agricultural land, the public announcement of the government of Havana a few years earlier, in 1991, to endorse the conversion of state-owned urban lots to agricultural production exemplified, at the level of the city, the reconfiguration of land tenure patterns characteristic of the move toward decentralized food production. It also illustrated the accompanying shift toward a locality-centered approach to agriculture encouraged, among other things, by the need to cut down on transportation, made difficult by the shortage of gasoline.

Urban agriculture not only transferred food production responsibilities to the city but also turned everyone's attention to smaller spatial scales, such as the neighborhood, in ways that signaled an important reconfiguration of prior government practices. In the past, government-led mobilizations—including those in agriculture—had foregrounded the national territory. According to the Cuban sociologist Armando Fernández Soriano (1999), government plans then overlooked diversity and difference in favor of macro programs designed for universal application across the nation. The emphasis was on the large scale, the communal, and the national. Patriotic sentiments were encouraged over affinity for the immediate locality as "the neighbourhood and the [local] community became progressively subsumed under the national" (Fernández Soriano and Otazo Conde 1996, 226).

While in the early 1990s media reports that celebrated the rise of vegetable gardens in cities throughout Cuba conjured up the image of national unity, the official representations of the urban agriculture movement differed qualitatively from those associated with previous mobilizations for agricultural production. Whereas the old motto of agricultural mobilizations had evoked a national landscape and had celebrated the work "of the people, by the people, and for the people" (*del pueblo, por el pueblo y para el pueblo*), the official motto of the urban agriculture movement replaced "the people" with "the neighborhood." To this day, in signs posted outside institutions such as the Agricultural Consultation and Input Stores, as well as in publications, brochures, certificates of merit, and census stickers distributed by the MINAG (see Figure 1.2), one can read the message that this is production "of (or in) the neighborhood, by the neighborhood, and for the neighborhood" (*del [en el] barrio, para el barrio y por el barrio*).

The revised slogan, credited to Eugenio Fuster, the municipal president of the Urban Agriculture Department in Havana, denotes a substantial rethinking of primary food production in Cuba in terms of scale and localization. What the slogan hides, however, is the extent to which this kind of government-endorsed production, especially in the early 1990s, made individual citizens, rather than local communities or the state, responsible for ensuring food security.

A Matter of Survival: Relying on One's Own Efforts and Means
In a 1979 speech, Fidel expressed the views of the political leadership regarding the responsibilities of the socialist state:

> Before [the revolution] the most a citizen could aspire to was for the state to build a post office, a telegraph station. . . . Today, citizens think it is right to expect everything from the state . . . and they are correct. And this is precisely the result of a collectivist mentality, a socialist mentality. Today, they expect everything from the administrative apparatus, and above all, from the political apparatus that represents them. Today, they do not need to rely on their own efforts, and their own means, as in the past. The fact that people today expect everything from the state is in keeping with the socialist consciousness that the Revolution has created in them. (quoted in García Pleyán 1996, 186)

The onset of the Special Period forced a radical change in this position as the state—no longer able to provide fully for its citizens—encouraged people to help themselves by "relying on their own efforts and their

Figure 1.2. Ministry of Agriculture census door sticker
displaying the urban agriculture slogan.

own means." As summed up in a popular song, broadcast over radio and
television during the first years of the crisis in a campaign to encourage
people to get involved in urban agriculture, "Only he who sows maize
may eat corn" (Instituto Cubano de Radio y Televisión 1993).[6]

Emblematic of this push for self-provisioning was *El Libro de la
Familia* (The Family Manual), a book coedited by Raúl Castro and his
late wife, Vilma Espín, then head of the Federation of Cuban Women.
The book's chapters, which were published serially in the popular *Bohemia* magazine from 1991 to 1993, gave technical information on how
to create a domestic garden and included survival tips, such as how to
subsist an entire year on a crop of potatoes cultivated in one's home gar-

den. The objective was to prepare the population for survival with a bare minimum of resources under warlike conditions of total isolation. This projection, in the experience of many Cubans at the time, was rapidly becoming a reality.

In this context, it was individuals who were ultimately responsible for securing their own food. The government played only a supporting role, both facilitating inputs such as land and seeds to those who needed them and opening the way for domestic and international NGOs to contribute to the urban food production effort.

NGOs, External Assistance, and the Food Production Effort

With government funds almost depleted, Cuba opened its doors to international aid coming from nonprofit, nongovernmental organizations as well as governmental agencies and entities originating in capitalist countries. Some of these organizations were willing to work directly with government institutions. In the field of agriculture, for example, the German Agro Acción Alemana (AAA), in the mid-1990s, collaborated with the MINAG to provide garden tools to the then newly formed horticulturalist clubs of Havana (Pelayo 1995). Such collaborations, however, were not necessarily the preferred choice for international actors. For a number of reasons—including political biases and the fear of unnecessary red tape—international funders were sometimes reluctant to enter into direct collaboration with institutions representing the Cuban government. Aware of this situation, the government allowed for the creation of NGOs and granted more autonomy to those already in existence.

In 1992, the revision of the Constitution permitted cultural or scientific Cuban celebrities with a patrimony that would benefit larger society to start their own foundations and run their own projects in collaboration with foreign institutions. Taking advantage of this opening, in 1994 Antonio Núñez Jiménez, who had amassed an impressive collection of artifacts from his earlier scientific expeditions in Latin America, started his own foundation. A geographer and veteran of the revolutionary struggle who decades earlier had led the First Agrarian Reform, Núñez Jiménez had a long-standing interest in all things environmental and

hoped that his foundation would assist in the protection of the environment and the development of a healthier relationship between society
and nature.

Given its environmental mandate, the Fundación Antonio Núñez
Jiménez de la Naturaleza y el Hombre (FANJNH), originally known as
the Fundación de la Naturaleza y el Hombre (the Foundation for Nature
and Humanity), was a perfect match for organizations like the Australian Conservation Foundation (ACF). In association with the Australian-
based Green Team, the ACF was looking to train Cubans in the practice
of permaculture, a variety of sustainable agriculture accredited to Australians Bill Mollison and David Holmgren. For the ACF, the FANJNH
offered a number of advantages. First, it represented a way to circumvent
a government bureaucracy that could interfere with the timely transfer of
funds necessary for the implementation of its programs; second, it gave
the ACF an opportunity to better meet its institutional objectives by
engaging in small-scale, manageable projects aimed at working directly
with individual citizens and local communities that could be construed
as authentic representatives of civil society (Hearn 2008, 114–19).

After its initial collaboration with the ACF, the FANJNH received
financial assistance from other foreign institutions, including the International Development Research Centre of Canada and OXFAM United
Kingdom. This assistance allowed the FANJNH to make a significant
contribution to the urban agriculture field, alongside other Cuban
NGOs that engaged in similar international cooperation projects.
Among these organizations was the Cuban Association for Animal Production, the Cuban Council of Churches, and the Center for Exchange
and Reference for Community Initiatives (Centro de Intercambio y Referencia sobre Iniciativas Comunitarias, CIERIC), about which more
will be said later. While modest in their individual efforts, these organizations have, since the early 1990s, provided valuable training and,
at times, necessary production inputs to thousands of small-scale producers working out of patios and parcelas. They have not only worked
with people who might have never been reached by current government
institutions and programs but also provided many of them with the
opportunity and resources to develop their production sites while gain-

ing national and international recognition. Although always monitored by an institutional government counterpart, the work of these Cuban NGOs ultimately signaled the extent to which small-scale expressions of urban agriculture had come to rely on nonstate and nonlocal sources of assistance. In this respect, they represented a decentering of the state in key activities involved in achieving food security.

The shift away from centralized management of food production efforts was also reflected in the increased individual responsibility and incentives granted to those who produced food for sale. In an attempt to "untie the knots" perceived to hold back productivity, the government now allowed the workers of sites like organopónicos to receive material incentives for increased production outputs. Despite a political rhetoric that continued to uphold the value of working for "the greater good," government policies at this time redirected individual conduct away from the ideal of selfless sacrifice for the nation and toward a more pragmatic and self-interested stance that privileged not just personal survival but also private profit.

A Renewed Emphasis on Material Incentives

In 1997, on the tenth anniversary of the Organoponic Movement, Raúl Castro visited the organopónico on Fifth Avenue in Havana. A newspaper article reporting on the visit stated that as Raúl "watched over the organopónico . . . , he commented: 'It is imperative to undo the knots which limit productive forces.'" He continued: "There is a misunderstanding of what egalitarianism means. In socialism there is equality of rights, but the rest depends on personal effort. Each person must live in keeping with his/her contribution to society. . . . If someone, honestly and with his/her own sweat, makes 1,000 pesos a month [five times an average salary], and he is not stealing it from anyone, we have no reason to worry about this" (Pages 1997b). Here, the minister of the FAR was referring expressly to a new kind of production spearheaded in Havana by the organopónico on Fifth Avenue, which functioned like a regular workplace with salaried workers except that increased outputs were linked to increased profit. Whereas previously agricultural workers would have been paid a fixed salary regardless of their output, those

24

associated with high-yield organopónicos, like the one on Fifth Avenue, earned more money the more they produced.

The notion that personal material rewards were an appropriate and desirable way to encourage higher productivity and efficiency at the workplace had long been debated in revolutionary Cuba. The famous guerrilla fighter Ernesto Che Guevara was the strongest opponent of this practice, insisting that the *Hombre Nuevo* (New Man), as he baptized the ideal citizen of socialist Cuba, "would become a stranger to the mercantile side of things, working for society, and not for profit" (Dumont 1970, 52). Che had argued: "Individualism as such, as the isolated action of a person alone in a social environment, must disappear in Cuba. Individualism tomorrow should be the proper utilization of the whole individual at the absolute benefit of the community" (quoted in J. L. Anderson 1997, 479).

At various points during the 1960s, the 1970s, and the mid-1980s, for pragmatic as well as ideological reasons, the Cuban government had asserted the primacy of moral incentives in mobilizing citizens to work for the benefit of all. During the Special Period, however, few felt moral prerogatives alone would help motivate people in that direction. Raúl Castro and General Sio Wong were among those within the political leadership who publicly endorsed the measured and orderly application of material rewards to encourage individuals to engage in efficient food production in the city beyond self-provisioning. This applied not just to organopónicos created with the purpose of commercialization in mind but also to those urban parcelas that, given their size and efficiency in production terms, were in a position to commercialize their outputs.

Many within the MINAG were initially skeptical about such experiments since they believed that urban agriculture was a waste of time. Having been trained to think that industrialized agricultural production in the countryside was the only viable option, these individuals felt that, material incentives aside, urban lots, no matter how sizable or efficiently worked, could never meet the food needs of the population. Despite this prevalent skepticism, the few MINAG employees who advocated for the development of urban agriculture in the early 1990s, with the support of key revolutionary figures, were able to assert their visions for change. Rogelio, one of the four founding members of the Urban Agriculture Department in Havana, speaking about the creation of organoponic gardens as having marked the ultimate acceptance of the activity in the city, told me: "They [other MINAG employees] accused us of being mad the first time we suggested doing agriculture in the city. Important personalities accused us of being crazy, crazy, crazy! They even turned their backs on us. They called us the four madmen of the city. But we persevered and we succeeded."

Despite such celebratory statements, the push to make room for agriculture in the city was never fully embraced by all MINAG officials. The same could be said for those individuals who had official jurisdiction over urban space and for whom the activity of urban agriculture presented serious challenges, particularly when it required the use of sizable lots in core municipalities of the city that were considered better suited for other functions. In this regard, urban agriculture at times pitted those involved in city planning and renovation against key decision makers in the Urban Agriculture Department and the armed forces, whose primary concern was increased food production rather than good urban design.

Rethinking the Function and Use of Urban Space

Sitting in his office at the INRE, Sio Wong smiled as he told me how he had encountered opposition to the creation of the organopónico on Fifth Avenue from none other than Eusebio Leal, the well-known and influential official historian of the city who had the unusual privilege of being authorized by the Central Committee of the Communist Party to sign his own international cooperation agreements to renovate and revitalize the municipality of Habana Vieja—a major tourist attraction and a source of state revenue. Leal had apparently initially opposed the organopónico, telling Sio Wong that "where there should be flowers, there should not be heads of lettuce," but had eventually retracted his opposition, telling the general that he had succeeded in making lettuce plants look like flowers!

Weeks later, Leal himself shared a slightly different version of events with me. He stated that for aesthetic reasons he had at first requested that the general consider having a flower nursery rather than a vegetable garden, but that the general had arrived at a compromise, bordering his garden with ornamental plants. In Leal's rendition, General Sio Wong had not triumphed in convincing him of the floral-like beauty of lettuce but rather had hidden his lettuce plants behind a concealing wall of flowers.

As this example illustrates, those with official jurisdiction over the design and development of urban space rejected the notion of bringing food production into core municipalities because such activities were considered unsightly and out of place, particularly in the capital. From the specific perspective of urban planners, agriculture was also seen to compete with functions like housing and recreation, in ways that ran counter to established ideas of good urban development and design.

For years, the spatial visions of those working in the urban planning sector had centered on long-term planning and ultimate state control over space believed to be necessary for ensuring the orderly and rational development of the city. According to a colorful brochure advertising the 1984 master plan for Havana, which was in use before the 1989 crisis, future development was to include "the renovation of the city through the construction of new buildings; the modernization of water, electricity and gas works, the transportation system, retail networks, commercial and public services and areas for sports, recreation and culture" (Dirección Provincial de Planificación Física y Arquitectura Ciudad Habana 1984). No space was given in this master plan for agriculture beyond a few isolated cases in the city outskirts. This, of course, changed with the onset of the crisis. Then, city planners learned to accept the use of core urban land for primary food production.

As early as 1989, long before the MINAG created its Urban Agriculture Department in 1994, representatives from the city government, the urban planning sector, the architecture department, the city's garbage disposal agency, and the peasant sector formed a committee whose task was to identify "every inch" of land in the city that could be made available for cultivation. Among those participating on behalf of the urban planning sector was Graciela, an engineer who, years later, joined the FANJNH's permaculture team. She recalled the long hours she and others put into the mapping of available vacant lots. In this process, she told me, urban planners often voiced concerns about the way in which urban agriculture might compete with other city functions in the future. Still, questions that became important in later years—such as environmental sustainability—were not even on the table. Graciela remembered when Sio Wong approached the committee with his plans for the organoponic garden on Fifth Avenue. By then, she explained, the city had "run out of land" and the committee had started to consider the use of vacant lots that were not naturally suited to agriculture. The spot chosen by Sio Wong was one such place. His proposal stood out from the rest because it involved considerable state investment and carried the seal of approval of Raúl Castro himself. Not surprisingly, the committee gave the project the green light. Whatever reservations people might have had about it, they set them aside to help address the food security crisis that by then was hitting Havana particularly hard.

By 2001, food security was no longer the most pressing issue in the country, but urban agriculture had become an established activity, now even officially incorporated into the city's new master plan. Many in the urban planning sector now conceded that larger sites, like organopónicos, made an important contribution to urban food security while smaller ones, like patios and parcelas, could play an important social and environmental function at the neighborhood level. Still, a map and accompanying planning guidelines (*lineamientos*) produced in 2001 by the Provincial Headquarters of Urban Planning betrayed a continued bias within the sector reflecting the presumption that "true" agriculture involved large-scale production and required large tracts of traditional cultivable land that could not be found in core areas of the city. Indeed, the guidelines unequivocally stated that the municipality of Playa, where Sio Wong's organopónico is located, as well as the municipalities of Habana Vieja and Centro Habana, where some of the growers I knew had had vegetable gardens for nearly a decade, were not suited for agriculture and could "*only* support silviculture in front yards and urban parks" (emphasis mine). For all the official pronouncements supporting urban agriculture, then, the urban planning sector appeared to remain at best ambivalent about the activity.

As shown in this chapter, the shift to urban agriculture required important revisions to established ways of envisioning both urban and agricultural space, as well as food provisioning, within socialist Cuba. These revisions were differently welcomed by state actors depending on their institutional affiliations and training but, in the end, even those who were reluctant understood the political import that urban agriculture held for the government as long as food security remained a problem in Havana. The next chapter explores the explicitly political dimension of related sites, considering how they have been both celebrated as "trenches for the revolution" and suspected as unruly spaces in need of state regulation and control.

2

Urban Agriculture, Politics, and Unwanted Deviations

Food, the Revolution, and Its Leadership

In 1997, I was invited by an employee of the FANJNH to join a group of foreign garden activists on a tour of Havana gardens. One of our first stops was the Santovenia home for the elderly, run by a group of Spanish nuns, in the humble municipality of El Cerro. Pastorita Núñez, a recent resident of the retirement home and a well-known revolutionary figure, greeted us at the gate, welcoming us to a small organopónico she had started there a few years prior. The garden provided the retirement home, as well as a couple of institutional kitchens in the neighborhood, with needed condiments and greens. Given Pastorita's status as a political celebrity, still remembered by many Cubans for her role in building and allocating homes at the beginning of the revolution, I was not surprised by the garden's already established fame. Pastorita was proud of the garden and seemed particularly pleased with the flowers growing around its perimeter, remarking that there was no reason vegetable gardens could not make room for beauty.

I did not see Pastorita again until June 2002. By then, her health had declined considerably and she had lost much of her earlier vitality. As we sat in the cloister of the Santovenia convent, she seemed somewhat distant, yet she politely responded to all my questions. When I asked her about the origins of the garden, she succinctly told me, "Being a revolutionary, once I heard Raúl Castro's speech on the radio complimenting those who were producing food against all odds, proving that

30

"*sí, se puede*" [yes, it can be done], I sent him a message and requested assistance to begin the garden." Raúl complied and the garden became a reality. As a newspaper article reported, Pastorita soon acknowledged Raúl's assistance by publicly naming him "godfather" of the site (Rodriguez Calderón 1995).

Pastorita was not alone in tracing the origins of her garden to the figure of Raúl Castro, then vice president of Cuba and minister of the FAR. General Sio Wong also mentioned Raúl in connection to the INRE garden, recounting to me how, as early as 1987, Raúl had directed the army to ensure its food provisions by creating organopónicos throughout the country. Sio Wong told me that, in 1991, as party members were called to intervene creatively to help fight the rising food insecurity among the population, he remembered Raúl's mandate of a few years back and applied it to Havana, creating the organopónico on Fifth Avenue.

The political pedigree of such urban agriculture sites was often mentioned in the media and was common knowledge among urban agriculture practitioners. It importantly hinted at the intimate connections of this practice as a whole with the revolutionary elite, embodied in the figure of Raúl, who was often described by higher-level officials within the FAR and the MINAG as the driving force behind the national urban agriculture movement.

There is no denying that, in Cuba, the rise of urban agriculture activities in the early 1990s was not only enabled but also promoted by the highest levels of government. Without the willingness of the leadership to allocate state land and ensure the widespread distribution of other necessary resources, such as production inputs, the urban agriculture movement would not have flourished as it has. It is also true that in a situation of extreme food insecurity, the political leadership could not afford to ignore the needs of the population, particularly in a country like Cuba, where food and politics are inextricably intertwined.

Drawing on narratives that represent the official perspective on urban agriculture, this chapter illustrates the manner in which related sites are discursively associated with the revolutionary struggle. The analysis further shows how, despite the talk of revolutionary commitment in this realm, in official circles urban agriculture is also recognized as posing serious challenges for established revolutionary tenets and institutionally entrenched modes of operating. As will be shown, concern over the unmonitored development of urban agriculture only increased as the economy recovered and state actors regained their ability to assert more centralized models of development. Before delving into the current political significance of urban agriculture, the chapter begins by explaining how, beginning in the early 1960s, food in Cuba became both a weapon and a casualty in an ideological war fought over the nation's right to assert its economic and political autonomy.

Food: A Weapon and a Casualty in an Ideological War
Beginning in February 1962, when the 1960 U.S. trade embargo on Cuba was expanded after Fidel publicly declared the socialist nature of *la revolución*, food became the first casualty in a political and economic war waged against the revolutionary government. Before the 1959 revolution, imports constituted a third of all food consumed in Cuba, and 70 percent of imported foodstuffs came from the United States (Boorstein 1968; Benjamin, Collins, and Scott 1986). In this context, the U.S. embargo delivered a severe blow to Cuba's food supply until the country set up regular trade relations with Soviet bloc countries. When these agreements began to dissolve in 1989, the U.S. embargo made its presence felt once again. Strengthened in 1996 through the Helms–Burton Act, which extended trade restrictions with Cuba to third-party countries,[1] the obstacles the embargo placed on Cuba's purchases of food and agricultural inputs in the world market only exacerbated food insecurity.[2]

Yet the impact of U.S. hostility toward Cuba in the area of food has not been limited to the embargo. Since the early 1960s, Cuba's agricultural sector has been a continuing target of U.S.-based biological warfare.[3] From 1962 to 1996, the Cuban government documented over eighteen such cases, including the introduction of a swine fever virus in 1979 and 1980 that led to the mass slaughter of three hundred thousand pigs, greatly affecting the consumption of pork, a key ingredient in the national diet. Against such a historical backdrop, it is easy to see how food production within Cuba, especially in times of acute food insecurity, would be conceived as an act of national defense.

Trabajo de cada uno
para disfrute de todos
En estos tiempos de resistir
un huerto también es revolución.

DALE COMO ES...

**Figure 2.1. Early advertisement promoting
urban agriculture. Source:** *Bohemia* **magazine.**

As early as 1991, when the city government of Havana, following directives from the Fourth Party Congress, rapidly allocated human and material resources (including land) to encourage individual citizens to engage in food production, public discussions of these efforts were presented as part of the struggle to defend the country and its political project. Thus, a poster appearing in the official magazine *Bohemia* in 1993 (see Figure 2.1) showed a generic garden being tilled by a woman and two men with an accompanying message: "Do it as it should be done: The contribution of each for the enjoyment of all. In these times of resistance, a *huerto* [vegetable garden plot] also means Revolution."

This linking of urban gardens with the defense of the revolution was still current nearly a decade later when one of the producers present at the First Annual National Meeting of the Patio and Parcela Movement, which took place in Havana on September 13, 2001, enthusiastically expounded: "What urban agriculture is doing is confronting a series of limitations that the people have taken on in defense of their own interests. We are happy to be in this movement for it is a battle trench from which we can also defend *la revolución*."[4]

While the use of war metaphors here fits a rhetorical style that has characterized other mass mobilizations in revolutionary Cuba—from literacy efforts to health campaigns—the above-mentioned history made military language particularly suitable to describe urban agriculture efforts. In the early years of the crisis, week after week the state media likened vegetable gardens to "war trenches" and "battlegrounds," garden produce to "cannons" and "ammunition," and gardeners to "troops" and "battalions" as the activity of urban food production was conceived as "the people's war."[5]

For all the applicability of war imagery in this context, however, more was required to mobilize the population. It was necessary to inspire people to think beyond the current bleak circumstances, to encourage them to be creative in finding the silver lining in what appeared to be ominous storm clouds. Urban agriculture here was presented as that silver lining.

The Language of Mobilization: "It Can Be Done"

During the crisis of the 1990s, the message that the duty of revolutionaries was to resist by struggling against all obstacles came to be encapsulated in the slogan *Sí Se Puede* (yes, it can be done!). This slogan was launched by Raúl in 1994 in the very speech that inspired Pastorita to begin her garden, which she fittingly baptized *Los Ancianos También Pueden* (the elderly also *can do it*). Speaking on the anniversary of the 1953 Moncada attack (July 26), Raúl explained how back then his brother, Fidel, had first exemplified how one could turn setbacks into victories. In Raúl's account, while the Moncada attack had failed in military terms, those who survived it, like Fidel, refused to surrender their ideals and turned the apparent defeat into an opportunity to inform people about the revolutionary project, rallying support for the struggle that would finally triumph in 1959. Raúl went on to explain that "the consistent lesson taught by Fidel is that 'It Can Be Done,' that people are capable of rising above the harshest conditions if their will to win does not fail" (Castro Ruz 1994a, 8).

This message, in another form, had been embraced by the Cuban media since 1991, when the *Tribuna de La Habana* newspaper began publishing a regular column on urban agriculture, with the cooperation of the MINAG, titled Sembrando Voluntad (Cultivating Willpower). But it was the slogan *Sí Se Puede*, not initially used to apply to urban agriculture per se, that became a sort of motto for the state-endorsed urban agriculture movement and permeated the speech of its participants. Even the magazine put out by the FANJNH in the mid-1990s, which, among other things, aimed to promote sustainable agriculture in the city, incorporated the slogan. The magazine was initially titled *Se Puede* (It Can Be Done) and later rebaptized *Se Puede Vivir en Ecópolis* (One Can Live in *Ecópolis*).

At the 2001 First Annual National Meeting of the Patio and Parcela Movement, the slogan, still in use, appeared over and over again on the lips of both organizers and producers, whether referring to their own specific gardens, those within the city of Havana, or more broadly those of the entire nation. A producer commented, "Those who have visited my house are surprised to find that everywhere there is a plant, in every crook and cranny; *it can be done.*" Contino enthusiastically declared, "The capital has earned for herself the right to receive food from other places because it does not have more land to produce everything for itself but it is showing, through example, that *it can be done!*" Adolfo Nodals (known as Adolfito), the national president of the Urban Agriculture Department, on recounting his recent visits to hundreds of gardens in the country, enthusiastically expounded: "We have seen things that show the wisdom, innovativeness, and intelligence of our people. We have seen incredible things, organopónicos in narrow house corridors, cultivation in drainage pipes, all kinds of variants, things that make you say, 'Man, how can this be possible? But *it can be done!*'"

The extent to which this official slogan became absorbed in the popular lexicon is further illustrated by a media report that tells the story of a twelve-year-old boy in the eastern province of Granma who started a successful garden in 1998 and baptized it "The Pioneers [revolutionary schoolchildren] Also *Can Do It!*" (*Los pioneros también pueden*) (Castro Medel 2001). This name, which, in generational terms, diametrically opposes the name Pastorita gave her garden in 1994 (The Elderly Also *Can Do It*), once again underscores the connection of some urban agriculture sites with the resistance efforts led by the revolutionary elite.

In this manner, a slogan coined by the minister of the Revolutionary Armed Forces (since 2008, the president of Cuba), emphasizing collective determination against all odds, helped discursively weave the relatively autonomous and localized efforts of individual citizens into what appeared as the unified struggle of an "imagined community" (B. Anderson 1991) of loyal socialist citizens. The connection between urban agriculture and political survival was evident to many, particularly the ruling elite.

Beans Are More Valuable Than Guns

In 1994, one of the worst years of the economic crisis, Raúl opened the National Assembly by proclaiming, "At this point in time . . . the central strategic, economic, political, ideological and military task for all Cuban revolutionaries, without exception, is to guarantee the population's food supply." Referring to the leading role that the Cuban Revolutionary Army had played in food production since before the economic crisis, Raúl further expounded, "Yesterday, we said that beans were as important as guns; today we are affirming that beans are more valuable than guns" (Castro Ruz 1994b, 12).[6] That this pronouncement came after popular demonstrations of discontent in the town of Cojímar and the municipality of Regla in July and September 1993, respectively, was no coincidence. As pointed out by experts on the subject, the Cuban Revolutionary Army did not have a history of involvement in direct repression of its own population, and this was not about to change. Rather than engaging in outright repression, the government attempted to address internal discontent through reforms geared at the restoration of food and welfare rights (Amuchastegui 2000). As Raúl's 1994 public speech underscored, food production was no longer the prerogative of a specialized sector of the population; it had become the prerogative of all "good revolutionaries," the means through which the struggle against adversity would have to be waged.

In this context, the encouragement of urban agriculture was not just about ensuring adequate access to food but, from the perspective of the political leadership, it was also about ensuring the government's continued legitimacy. In 2001, General Sio Wong plainly told me, "The work of urban agriculture is the best political work one can do; the cadre who does not understand this is of no use." He solemnly added, "Urban agriculture is food for the people." Along similar lines, Contino, national president of the CDRs, at the First Annual National Meeting of the Patio and Parcela Movement, explained that the promotion of urban agriculture "is a job born for the CDRs since it involves the defense of the revolution. It is a job for revolutionary vigilance insomuch as we watch over the situation to ensure that our people are well fed." He further pronounced, "A good revolutionary must know what he has to do in this field."

Precisely how a good revolutionary should behave in this field was hotly debated at this time. Despite the constant public associations of urban agriculture with the revolutionary struggle, a general feeling circulated among officials that some of the changes implemented through urban agriculture could lead the population astray. In fact, some aspects of the activity were thought to need urgent control if urban agriculture was to remain an officially endorsed practice in Havana. As will become evident in the next section, the concerns here were as much about the efficient, legal, and rational use of space as about the dangers of allowing a sector of civil society to distance itself from key revolutionary values and, importantly, from the state control apparatus.

Guarding Revolutionary Achievements: Dangerous Ruptures

On June 14, 2002, I was invited to attend an event for those involved in the Agricultural Consultation and Input Stores (Tiendas Consulto-rios Agropecuarios, TCAs). The event was to offer an insider's evaluation of the work of the forty-eight TCAs then operating in all municipalities of the city. These stores, located on state land, were created to serve small-scale producers by providing them with easy access to agricultural inputs, such as seeds, sold with a modest markup price.[7] The Agricultural Input Enterprise (Empresa de Suministros Agropecuarios, ESA), a subdivision of the MINAG, provided TCAs with these price-protected products. TCA staff did not receive salaries but worked on commission primarily derived from the sale of nonprotected items (e.g., ornamental plants and gardening tools), which they procured independently of ESA and could price as they wished. Although TCA staff had to share a portion of their profits with ESA, their business was profitable, with the income of TCA employees doubling that of the average national salary (Cruz Hernández and Sánchez Medina 2001).

The meeting opened with an esoteric paper about pyramidal energy and the positive impact it can have on agricultural production. Sitting at the head table were Alfredo Gutiérrez, the vice-minister of agriculture; Evelio González, the new director of the ESA; Alfredo Rubio, the new head of the Metropolitan Horticultural Enterprise; and, last but not least, Eugenio Fuster Chepe, the provincial president of the Urban Agriculture Department for the city of Havana. I had heard a lot about Fuster and had attempted, unsuccessfully, to interview him for months. He spoke with an admonishing tone to the audience. As if to reaffirm his materialist leanings and disassociate himself from the opening paper on pyramidal energy, he began by saying, "Now more than ever we need to have our hands and our feet firmly planted on the ground." The meeting soon took on the air of an accountability trial, with Fuster calling up the municipal delegates of agriculture, in charge of supervising and supporting the work of the TCAs, to report on the failures of these institutions' administrators and employees, who were also in attendance.

At times Fuster confronted one person with another, publicly shaming a few, including Papito, a model TCA administrator who, according to Fuster, almost lost his license when he was found selling honey at the store (TCAs are supposed to sell inputs for agricultural production, not agricultural products). Fuster commented on the irony that this happened in the home district of the first socialist community in Cuba, the locality where "everything [having to do with private enterprise] was first eliminated." The warnings were valid, he added, "lest Papito now think of instituting private property at this locality's TCA!" Fuster clearly delivered the message that the actions of Papito and others like him could jeopardize the very existence of the TCAs. "The future of the TCAs is in everybody's hands," he continued. "We can develop them to their full positive potential, just as we can suddenly dissolve all of them because they have deviated from their social objective [*objecto social*]." As if to drive the point home again, he underscored, "The TCA is not a business; it is a technical information center; it is not a store."

Inasmuch as they commercialized their stock, the TCAs did appear to deserve the label "stores," yet as Evelio, the new director of ESA, had already told me during an interview, the TCAs were being rebaptized once again. The word *tienda*, meaning store, which then stood first in the name Tiendas Consultorios Agropecuarios, was switching places with Consultorios (Consultation Center), emphasizing instead the service and noncommercial dimensions of the site (see Figure 2.2). This renaming, which was in keeping with Fuster's message, had already been effected in some of the signs marking the stores. However, in an act that appeared to challenge (and even undo) the intent of the official reordering of names, these new signs sometimes depicted the word *tienda*, now taking second place in the name, in much larger letters than the other words.

Figure 2.2. Old and new logos for Agricultural Input Stores.

As I sat at the TCA self-evaluation meeting, spoken and written messages also appeared to me to subvert one another. The banner that hung behind the table set up for the speakers read "Full steam ahead to December of 2002, undoing knots. Yes, *it can be done*!!—Raúl Castro." When I thought back to General Sio Wong's explanation that "the undoing of knots" phrase referred to the overcoming of prejudices against linking productivity to profit, Fuster's current comments warning that "TCAs are not for profit" appeared to contradict the banner behind him, although, clearly, the distinction was one between honest profit regulated by the state and profiteering connected to illegal activities.

Figure 2.3.
Nonprotected
items for sale at an
Agricultural Input
Store.

Toward the end of the meeting, Fuster clarified this position while alluding to Raúl's statement about the acceptability of honest profit ("he who makes 1,000 pesos . . ."). Fuster commented, "Our wish is that the average salary for TCA staff be 1,000 pesos . . . but this cannot be achieved purely by selling hammers." In other words, the TCAs cannot get rich by selling unauthorized items, such as honey, or by selling only nonprotected items, like agricultural tools (see Figure 2.3), from which they stand to profit the most (there is no ceiling for markup on these items). They also have to engage equally in less profitable activities that support the endeavors of small-scale farmers, such as the sale of seeds and technical literature. After all, the sale of protected items is the raison d'être of the TCAs (Cruz Hernández and Sánchez Medina 2001, 91). Fuster closed by saying: "Brain, heart, and pocket. We have to unite the three. There has to be a balance!"

A Fine Balance: Reasserting Community Solidarity
In the view of many, Special Period reforms undermined a previously existing solidarity among fellow Cubans so that, as suggested by Fuster's words, the drive for personal profit now appeared to override the need to contribute to the well-being of the broader society. At many of the institutional meetings I attended, as well as in media reports of the time, the productivity and generosity observed at some urban agriculture sites were praised while the greed and selfishness exhibited at others were harshly criticized. Some organopónicos were publicly denounced for breaking their agreement with the state by selling at prices not sufficiently below those of newly opened agricultural markets (Pages 1997a), selling beyond their local jurisdiction (Rodríguez and Ferrán 1996), and prioritizing sales to the tourist sector—all actions that increased profits at the expense of meeting the needs of neighborhood residents and local institutions, understood by most to be the intended beneficiaries of this kind of site.[8] That these deviations were perceived to be getting worse with the passage of time was made evident during an interview I conducted in May 2002 with a television journalist who specialized in urban agriculture. The journalist told me, "The objective [of organopónicos] was to serve a local community, to provide it with food, but they are too concentrated now on growing and growing; they have moved beyond their initial goal; they have distanced themselves from their social objective."

The overall message, reiterated in various contexts, was that just as the TCAs had been assigned a social objective that they had to fulfill above all else, urban food producers who had been authorized by the government to market their produce were expected to contribute in specific ways to society in return for the support received from the government, which had, among other things, authorized their use of urban land and allowed them to profit from sales (Bedriñana Isart 1996).

The principle that urban agriculture sites must serve a social objective and avoid profiteering was also applied to parcelas, which, as previously stated, are usually given in usufruct by the state. One of the founders of the Provincial Urban Agriculture Department in Havana told me: "There has to be legality in the use of the parcela land and the resources used for its exploitation, because everything has to have an order. It cannot degenerate into barbarism." By *barbarism* he was referring to the not-so-uncommon misuse of this public land for nonsanctioned activities aimed strictly at profiteering, such as renting the land as a parking lot or hiring labor to work on it for one's own benefit as if one were a *terrateniente* (powerful landowner) in prerevolutionary times.[9] While some parcelas were authorized to engage in sales, this did not mean that they should privilege profit over contribution to the broader community. One of the model producers present at the 2001 meeting of the Patio and Parcela Movement made a public statement in this regard, suggesting that those involved in sales were particularly susceptible to the temptation of profiteering. Referring to the work done on his parcela, he explained:

> It is nice to speak of the variety of production in a patio or par-cela. I would add that it is also nice to speak of production thinking about it in relation to our pockets, but it is even more important to prioritize the population more than our pockets. We must think in which ways we are going to better benefit the population and better serve its needs. In our case, we benefited more economically being a fruit tree nursery than producing vegetables. However, we realized that the surrounding population benefited more from the latter and hence we have turned to that.

Narratives like this one show how Fuster's balancing triad of "brain, heart, and pocket" is publicly foregrounded as central to the urban agriculture movement and the "proper" development of related sites. Through such narratives, the gamut of urban agriculture sites, from the small-scale parcelas to the high-yield organopónicos, emerge as spaces that ought to fortify rather than betray the "revolutionary" emphasis on solidarity with the broader community. As suggested by the final words of this producer, it is not just the unrestrained pursuit of profit that is officially decried as a deviation from revolutionary values: a general disconnection from the broader society is thought to be equally harmful and in need of correction.

Also seen from these same narratives, ensuring such solidarity and adherence to "social objectives" is not considered easy. In Fuster's view, the increasing momentum of productive forces "freed" during the Special Period threatened to drive behavior in less desirable directions. At the TCA meeting he warned, "Urban agriculture is like a locomotive that could run all of us to the ground." While years earlier Raúl Castro had summoned people in the movement to "move full steam ahead," now Fuster, no doubt following directives from above, used similar imagery to call for caution and control.

This notion that control had become necessary to ensure the proper development of urban agriculture was also shared—albeit for different reasons—by those in the urban planning sector who were officially responsible for the proper development of urban space.

Reordering Space: The Problem of Agriculture Out of Place
In May 2001, a meeting was organized at the office of the Group for the Holistic Development of the Capital (Grupo para el Desarrollo Integral de la Capital, GDIC) to discuss an upcoming book on urban agriculture and the development of local, sustainable economies. The venue was appropriate for the topic because GDIC had, since 1987, been working with the government of the city toward promoting participatory planning and community development. In attendance at the meeting were many key figures from the urban planning sector, including a high-level official from the National Urban Planning Office who angrily opened the discussion by commenting on the chaotic situation planners faced in the outskirts of Havana, where the Finca (Farm) Program, coordinated by the MINAG, was leading back to an undesirable fragmentation of agricultural landholdings and the "repeasantization" and reruralization of the population. This, she argued, was not only undoing the work carried out by the revolutionary government in earlier years but also complicating the work of urban planners in charge of ensuring the provision of

services, such as transportation and potable water, to the population at large. As she explained, the rational allocation of resources facilitated in the case of concentrated settlements was made only more difficult by the current dispersion of producers in space.

Others commented in general about the less than rational use of space that had accompanied the promotion of urban agriculture in all parts of Havana. A Cuban employee of Habitat Cuba started by saying, "It has happened that organopónicos have been built just because there was a nook here, a vacant lot there, even though they broke up the normal flow of city streets." An urban planner echoed the sentiment, saying, "There are many, in the city, who love to produce food, but this cannot be left to each person's desires." Along the same lines, another planner interjected, "It could be that urban agriculture is a city function, like housing, but gardens should be properly designed." Yet another wrapped up the thought, adding: "One gets a professional to design one's house and follows the urban regulations that apply to the urban area in question. With urban agriculture, it should be the same."

There seemed to be a general consensus that informal urban agriculture actions, initially taken (and encouraged) during the worst period of the crisis on both public and private lands, were in need of redress for infrastructural as well as for aesthetic reasons. The single Urban Agriculture Department official in attendance, Rogelio, sheepishly agreed that in the midst of the crisis urban agriculture sites "were located where they should not be," and now there was an urgent need to organize them and put some order into urban agriculture. This ordering, according to those present, would need to involve not just the possible relocation of organopónicos but also the relocation, dismantling, and closer regulation of the smaller-scale patios and parcelas. Indeed, this was in part the intention of the newly launched Patio and Parcela Movement, promoted by the MINAG and the CDRs, whose related census and competition for the title of model garden aimed to bring into view (and hence under control) those sites that already existed but were unaccounted for. This would allow MINAG officials to bring producers in line with standards for agricultural production in the city that emphasized the implementation of sustainable practices and would result in better integration of these sites into the urban fabric. Considering that of all urban agriculture sites parcelas and patios were not only the most numerous but also the most geographically dispersed and relatively independent of the state, this was a tall order.[10] Still, the integration of these sites was desirable not only to ensure adequate urban organization and promote proper agricultural practices but also to prevent the negative political implications of a citizenry that was perceived to have begun to act too independently from the state.

The Threat of Civil Society Thriving in Out-of-the-Way Places
I last saw Manuel in November 2008 at the Third Latin American Permaculture Convention organized by the FANJNH in Cuba. He was literally wrapped up in a vine he was exhibiting at a plant exchange, posing for a picture for a U.S. participant at the convention. Many, then, dismissed him as a madman, but those who knew him, regardless of their view of his increasingly eccentric behavior, respected him as a longtime defender of sustainable agriculture and community participation in Cuba. I had not seen him for many years, but he still remembered a long conversation we had in 2000, when he was living in the district of Santa Fé, in the municipality of Playa, a place that had acquired mythological proportions for those in the urban agriculture field.

In the early years of the crisis, Manuel, a practicing agronomist, had been appointed to act as the representative of the MINAG in the district of Santa Fé. Under his leadership and that of a couple of other residents with comparable charisma, gardening in Santa Fé had turned into a community-building activity that resulted in the creation of the first horticulturalist clubs and the first agricultural consultancy offices (a noncommercial precursor of the TCAs) in the city.[11] Manuel playfully labeled these initial years the "prehistory" of the urban agriculture movement, for they have been carefully silenced in recent official accounts that trace the origins of the activity not to its grassroots source but rather to institutional figures, like Adolfito, the current national president of the Urban Agriculture Department and head of the INIFAT (one of the agricultural research centers on the periphery of Havana).

Manuel, who for years worked with the community development

branch of the Cuban ecumenical group known as the Cuban Council of Churches, used religious metaphors throughout our interview. He likened Adolfito to the pope, the INIFAT to the Vatican, and his own previous activities as delegate of agriculture to those of a preacher or a priest of liberation theology embedded in his or her community and having no time for the "church hierarchy." His description of the transition between the "prehistory" and the "history" of the urban agriculture movement denoted a shift between a grassroots movement and direct community participation on the one hand, and formal bureaucratic structures and a distant official authority on the other.

Recounting the general atmosphere at the meetings of the original horticulturalist clubs, Manuel commented:

> The meetings were not the classic meetings where you sit down and an individual spends two hours telling you what you ought to do. There was an opportunity for you to be heard. At first, some [producers] were suspicious that they were being called to a meeting to report on their production and that then they would be told how much of this production they would have to give away [to the state]. Gradually, they realized that was not our objective.

From the perspective of frontline workers, like Manuel, as well as that of a number of Cuban intellectuals who closely followed developments in Santa Fé (Dilla, Fernández Soriano, and Castro Flores 1997; Fernández Soriano and Otazo Conde 1996; Fernández Soriano 1997, 1999), the urban agriculture movement had opened a new space for participation, redefining citizen involvement in a manner that could strengthen the socialist project and inject new life into *la revolución*. Such optimism was not shared by those used to what Manuel described as "top-down and very authoritarian political schemes: vices that had been created and reproduced by the system."

Some institutions with close links to the state, like the CDRs and the Federation of Cuban Women, initially felt threatened and disapproved of horticulturalist clubs that called independent meetings in the *barrios* (neighborhoods) without first properly informing the representatives of established mass organizations. According to Manuel, these institutions, which were created decades earlier to work with the population at the grassroots level, had fallen prey to "excessive institutionalization" that left no room for spontaneous participation from the population.[12]

This impulse toward "institutionalization," with its emphasis on hierarchical authority and tight controls, was, not surprisingly according to Manuel, reflected in the actions of formal state institutions, such as the MINAG, which soon suggested rebaptizing the representative of agriculture *Jefe de Área* (area chief).[13] The representatives of agriculture at the time rejected this title, imposed by the higher echelons of the MINAG, and fought to include at least the title "extension worker" in parentheses, alongside the title of chief, which for them had unpleasant authoritarian connotations. In fact, the name change was accompanied by a shift in job description expanding the role beyond supporting small-scale producers in their production endeavors, to incorporating a sort of "police" function that entailed monitoring producers' activities and even administering fines to those who violated MINAG rules regarding the use of usufruct land.

The emphasis on control did not disappear but rather intensified as the economy recuperated and the government became progressively concerned about all unregulated activities allowed to thrive in the initial years of the Special Period. A 1996 report of the political bureau, read publicly by Raúl Castro, made particular reference to these activities and their political implications. The report warned that any "openings" that deviated from the already established path exposed Cuba to "enemy subversion and external influences." These "external influences"—among which could be included the international funders of many new Cuban NGOs—were said to be working toward the creation of a "fifth column" (quoted in Hoffman 2000, 66–67).[14] The report advocated the rejection of further internal "openings," including the rise of individual enterprise or self-employment (*cuentapropismo*) that, in the words of the director of the Communist Party Cadre School, would amount to planting the seed for "a local bourgeoisie . . . that sooner or later would serve the counter-revolution" (ibid., 67).[15]

Before the reading of the 1996 report, the political mood in Cuba had changed considerably. Along with signs of a recovering economy, there had come a renewed escalation of tensions with the United States culminating in the Helms–Burton Act, which broadened the U.S. embargo to third-party countries. At this point, local NGOs, allowed to flourish at the beginning of the Special Period as a means to draw needed foreign currency into Cuba (Fernández Soriano 2001), not only were considered less necessary to the economic recovery of the country but also were perceived to be prone to political deviations. For these reasons, a freeze was placed on their creation, with existing NGOs reminded through example that dissolution would result if, as the 1996 report warned, they "deviated from the established path."

These measures, along with the institutionalizing policies of the MINAG, were to curtail the evolution of "novel" forms of community participation, such as those associated with the vegetable gardens (*huertos*) described by Manuel. Although the 1996 report of the political bureau did not directly refer to urban agriculture sites per se, it did explicitly and negatively allude to the work of those Cuban scholars (e.g., Dilla 1996) who had celebrated the opening of new participatory spaces within civil society associated, among other things, with neighborhood grassroots movements built around huertos. While informal networks continued to be created through urban agriculture activities, after 1996 most people understood that legitimate organizing and group action required affiliation with, and approval of, officially recognized state institutions or trusted NGOs—a situation that generally led many producers to voluntarily seek formal affiliation with a range of organizations that could give an official seal of approval to their activities.

From the perspective of those in official positions of authority—from agriculture representatives to urban planners to high-ranking government officials—urban agriculture in Havana, even when seen to represent desirable openings and exciting new developments by some, was received with considerable apprehension by many. As shown, public representations and practices of urban agriculture sites reflected disagreement and tension among pertinent Cuban state institutions and actors regarding the most desirable organization of this activity and its related spaces. Despite these tensions, by 2000, when material conditions had improved and the state had managed to recuperate some of its economic power, a coherent discourse and set of practices appeared to be emerging. Most institutional actors coincided in reasserting a previously hegemonic understanding of the ideal organization of space that emphasized order and central planning, reaffirming the ultimate power of the state. Sometimes, this power was reasserted in reference to the primacy of revolutionary ideals that underscored solidarity with the broader community, while at other times, it was mere adherence to official regulations and rules that appeared to matter most.

As will be seen, producers working in this field understood these expectations and, whether out of conviction or as a result of political maneuvering, in their own public practices and discourses reproduced the ideal of solidarity with the wider community, adherence to officially endorsed agricultural practices, and their ultimate allegiance to *la revolución*. Still, as illustrated in the following chapter, for producers associated with patios and parcelas, involvement in food production was generally driven by personal and mundane desires and objectives. Their practice was largely private, and their politics was, above all, a politics of necessity shaped by shifting landscapes of power that left them feeling marginalized from a rapidly changing Cuban economy. Their perspective on patios and parcelas spoke of a lived experience of these sites seldom acknowledged in official discourses.

3

Place-Bound

Becoming an Urban Farmer in Havana

I was first introduced to Manolo, a rabbit breeder from the humble municipality of El Cerro, in early 2001, when Havana was changing so rapidly I never knew what to expect on each visit. Every time I returned someone I knew had left Cuba in search of a better life overseas; new hotels, restaurants, and hard-currency stores had appeared in places where none had existed before; and the old American cars that once dominated the roads seemed increasingly outnumbered by new imports. Among the few things that remained constant for me over the next decade were Manolo's hospitality and the decor of his sparsely furnished living room: his bike parked in a corner, a hard sofa, and a couple of rocking chairs placed in a semicircle to one side; on one wall, a large framed picture of Jesus; on the other, two pictures from his fishing days.

One afternoon, as we chatted about life, he pointed to the fishing pictures and told me that he had owned a boat for many years and, had he wanted to, he could have left Cuba but, he explained, "I am not interested in leaving. I am not interested in living elsewhere, particularly not the U.S. I would like to go to Canada but the climate is too harsh." He laughed and continued: "Spain, I don't like it either. Besides, I don't have to go anywhere; my neighbors, my neighborhood, this is my family. The neighbors have known me since I was a child. Do you understand? Why would I want to go anywhere where people don't even know who I am? Here everyone knows me and I am a popular guy."

Manolo did not mention any hardships at the beginning of our conversation, but later he did touch on the issue of food scarcity several times. When he discussed why people had, since the early 1990s, turned in greater numbers to cultivating vegetable gardens or breeding rabbits at home in a place like Havana, he summed up the situation with the following words: "Household heads in particular feel the necessity of feeding their young. So it is they who sacrifice themselves by entering this world [of urban agriculture]."

Although some Cubans—aided by new lucrative work in the tourist industry, remittances, or new work and study opportunities overseas—were able to fend off (or altogether escape) the worst effects of the still lingering crisis, not everyone was so lucky.[1] For many Havana residents, the "new" global sense of place mentioned in the Introduction was paired up with feelings of scarcity, despair, and isolation. For many of the people I worked with, their world shrank rather than expanded as Cuba supposedly opened to the world; their feeling of being rooted in place was not erased but ironically amplified as myriad transnational flows of people, ideas, capital, and goods increasingly crisscrossed national boundaries. While in some ways the urban farmers I worked with appeared to be quintessential postmodern subjects that "have entered into a new condition of neighborliness, even with those most distant from [themselves]" (Appadurai 1990, 2), they remained remarkably place-focused and, most of all, place-bound.

This chapter sketches how small-scale urban agriculture practitioners associated with parcelas and patios experience their neighborhood, and their production sites, and how this experience, in turn, connects to citizens' experience of changing material circumstances during the Special Period. So far as this chapter considers the everyday, nonpublicized, and even underground narratives and experiences of small-scale producers pertaining to the spaces they inhabit, it not only begins to reveal the lived dimension of parcelas and patios but also throws light on the perspective of a segment of civil society seldom given a voice in official narratives within Cuba and also largely ignored in the international literature that celebrates Cuban urban agriculture.[2]

The analysis reveals common, as well as divergent, perspectives among practitioners on the significance of parcelas and patios and their ideal relationship with the broader community and the state. In addition to illustrating the privatization of public spaces involved in the making of parcelas, the analysis shows the impact that the gardens in general have on producers' sense of well-being and their feeling of connectedness to the world around them. These feelings, as will be seen, often contrast with producers' experience of the surrounding human community and physical environment.

In contrast with prior chapters that focused on public narratives and official practices pertaining to urban agriculture sites, which explicitly underscore their political significance and supposed role in a changing socialist Cuba, this chapter focuses on the individual and lived dimensions of these sites and their connection to personal and mundane needs. From this perspective, parcelas and patios emerge as distinctive spaces that allow for the pursuit of personal rather than political or national projects—although it would be wrong to assume that these two need to be exclusive of each other. Indeed, as subsequent chapters will show, projects that are primarily personal and have no explicit political agenda do converge with state projects and, on occasion, partake in reproducing ideals previously promoted by the socialist state.

Enclosing Scales and the Practice of Urban Agriculture

Manolo finished his commentary on people's recent involvement in urban agriculture by saying, "Besides, now, household heads do not go out anyway; now, there are no buses to go anywhere; there are no places to go out to, so they keep themselves entertained this way [by becoming involved in primary food production at home]." Manolo was not exaggerating. Not only had recreational places still accessible to Cubans greatly deteriorated, but transportation to them was limited. For the majority of urban farmers I worked with, moving even short distances within the city was, until recently, an onerous and uncomfortable task.

During the initial years of the economic crisis, Havana experienced acute shortages of gasoline and replacement parts for motor vehicles. Car traffic, which had always been fairly limited in postrevolutionary Cuba (Schweid 2004), dropped by a third from its pre-1989 levels. Havana's public transportation system, which had once consisted of ap⊦ mately two thousand buses that moved four million people a day, can₁ to a near halt and recuperated too slowly in subsequent years to keep up with demand.[3] By 2001, when Manolo made his comment, buses were too crowded and the lines for them too long to make them a viable option for many people. The great majority of those I worked with moved around on foot or by bicycle—a mode of transportation that had become common at the peak of the economic crisis.[4] Their limited mobility was reinforced in most cases by their status as retired or unemployed people who, no longer obliged to go out to work, spent most of their day at home or nearby.[5]

Provisions through the state-subsidized ration stores located in every neighborhood had previously adequately covered basic food needs, but now they met only 55 percent of an individual's nutritional requirements (Díaz Vázquez 2000). Although since the beginning of the post-1989 crisis new food supply venues had opened up throughout the city, access was far from universal. Above the ration quotas, common items, such as chicken and eggs, generally had to be purchased in dollar stores—opened in 1993—at prices that were still high for most people. For example, chicken legs were sold for a dollar a pound, which then equaled approximately one-eighth of an average monthly salary.[6] The variety and quality of produce available at *agromercados*—the agricultural markets where, since 1994, independent farmers and members of cooperatives have been allowed to sell directly to the population—varied from one neighborhood to another, with those located in more affluent areas better stocked. In general, most agromercados offered root crops like cassava, fruits like plantains, and meat such as pork and goat, but prices for these items remained high for average peso-earning citizens, sometimes costing them ten times the price they would have paid for the same through the ration. Some animals, such as rabbits, were not sold at agromercados but instead at a few expensive restaurants in well-to-do neighborhoods.

Small-scale urban agriculture, practiced in home patios or neighborhood vacant lots, offered people access to rabbits, chickens, eggs, and a range of vegetables they could not easily get otherwise. From this perspective, engagement in primary food production was understandably experienced less as a choice than, as Manolo put it, a necessity experienced by those lacking the required financial resources or mobility to take advantage of existing food venues. Here, the practice of urban agriculture emerged not as an action taken in defense of *la revolución*, or even the nation, but as a personal choice for survival in a context of uneven food access.

Partly originating out of restricted mobility, urban agriculture itself also resulted in increased immobility for practitioners as the activities involved in properly caring for plants and animals required them to remain in place. While small-scale urban farmers told me they found pleasure in their food production endeavors, they also described the work involved with terms such as *mucho sacrificio* (much sacrifice) and *un trabajo esclavo* (an enslaving job), emphasizing how their work tied them to the production site (usually located in or near the home), preventing travel for long periods of time.

Being restricted to life in the barrio was experienced negatively by some of the producers. Their descriptions of their barrios—particularly in the core municipalities of El Cerro, La Habana Vieja, and Centro Habana, where I conducted the bulk of my research—betrayed a sense of feeling enclosed within a decaying physical and social environment that was perceived to have deteriorated particularly as a result of the economic crisis and general lack of resources available for construction, urban development, and employment opportunities. The physical surroundings were often described as "decaying" and "dilapidated" and as lacking in pleasant public spaces. While producers did interact with their neighbors and, as indicated by Manolo's words, were close to some of them, they considered themselves to be different from most barrio residents.

Producers defined themselves as "hardworking," "honest," and "law-abiding" people who minded their own business and were easy to get along with. Although most, like Manolo, had trusted friends in their neighborhood, it was not uncommon for producers to describe the majority of residents in the barrio as being of dubious character. Speaking of his neighbors, Roberto, a self-employed mechanic in his midthirties who had been raising chickens and rabbits with the help of his wife on the rooftop of his childhood home, went so far as to say: "To be honest, I prefer a total stranger to the Cuban next to me because it is the latter who is harming me; he is the one who wants to steal my animals, who gossips about me buying feed [illegally]. Since they do not have much to eat, they speak ill of you behind your back. These things bother you because you are sacrificing yourself, working hard, and they are gossiping behind your back."

In addition to highlighting awareness of growing inequalities in the area of food access and the tensions arising from that situation within the neighborhood, this and other narratives underscored the uncomfortable feeling of "being watched"—a feeling related to a history of surveillance formally embedded in nationwide, neighborhood-based civic organizations such as the CDRs, whose functions included reporting on counterrevolutionary or "antisocial" activities. The CDRs, located on every city block, have in recent years reputedly become less effective at monitoring the activities of neighborhood inhabitants. Nevertheless, some residents—based on prior experience with this organization—continue to feel that each neighbor is a potential state informant. In this sense, some of the producers seemed to experience the small territorial unit of the neighborhood as a sort of "public stage" where they could not afford to be totally open and had to manage their image. Whether they were buying agricultural inputs on the black market or breaking some known rules regarding food production in the city, most producers felt neighbors had the power to get them into trouble with authorities, potentially leading to the halting of their agricultural practices. While in this respect producers felt they had to be mindful of what they did at their production sites, they also felt safest and most at ease when they were there. This is not surprising considering that most of these sites, even those located on state land, were treated and experienced as private spaces.

Creating Private Places on State Land

Sitting in the crowded bedroom-studio of his tiny three-room house in El Cerro, about six blocks from Roberto's house, Pedro, a man in his late fifties, succinctly recounted how he and his neighbors had created four gardens on a demolition site adjoining their residences on Dawn Street. He recalled, "We took out all the garbage and sealed the façade of the building so that no one could dump garbage into the site." This "sealing off" made the gardens both inaccessible and invisible from the street (see Figures 3.1 and 3.2). In addition to the obvious practical reasons for this enclosure (preventing vandalism and theft, damage by animals, etc.), this action effectively excluded surrounding community members from a space that had previously been open to everyone. In this sense, the fenc-

Figure 3.1. Makeshift facade for garden site on Dawn Street (view from the street).

Figure 3.2. Location of garden site on Dawn Street (view from the alleyway).

Figure 3.3. Private gate for one of the gardens on Dawn Street.

Figure 3.4. Another private gate for one of the Dawn Street gardens.

ing of this and other parcelas in the city signaled the de facto appropriation of a public, common space by private citizens.

This "privatization" of public land through its conversion into parcelas was further underscored by the creation or placement of physical connectors between the garden sites and the private residences of their caretakers. Thus, in Pedro's alley, each garden doorway was specifically carved out to more or less face the entrance doors of the private residences of the gardeners located a meter away across the alley (see Figures 3.3 and 3.4). Beyond the obvious convenience of this arrangement, this positioning of doorways and even windows (see Figure 3.5) spatially underscored the intimate relationship understood to exist between the caretakers' residences and the gardens. That the latter were experienced as an extension of the domestic space was evident in the way in which parcela caretakers or *parceleros* often referred to these sites as their home patios. Thus, Román, a neighbor of Pedro's described his residence to me by saying: "My house is composed of a small living room, a kitchen, a washroom, a room I built upstairs, and my patio [referring to the parcela]. . . . I opened a little door there in the patio right across from mine so that, although it is in a separate lot, it is really part of my home." Pedro had gone even further in spatially marking the parcela as part of his property. Taking advantage of the fact that his home was the last one in the alley, he placed a wooden fence not just across the garden's doorway but across the alley itself, effectively enclosing his residence and the parcela opposite to it into a single spatial unit.

Physical markers like this, which spatially denote the incorporation of the parcela into the producer's private home, were not uncommon in the city. Although they are impossible with parcelas located far from the producer's residence, when physical proximity permits, such links are often made. Thus, a parcela in Habana Vieja that adjoined the back wall of the producer's residence, although the entrance was on a parallel street one block over, was symbolically marked by a dangling string of aluminum cans functioning as scarecrows, which stretched from the producer's home terrace to the garden lot below. The planned addition of permanent fixtures in many of the parcelas I visited, as well as the plant-

Figure 3.5. A view of Pedro's garden from his home window.

ing of long-term crops, further suggests a sense of ownership rights on the part of parceleros.

These private claims are also reflected by the presence of furnishings and objects that further incorporate these places into the domestic sphere of the producers. Parcelas are often used by the caretakers and their families to store private household goods or for activities like hanging the laundry to dry. They also contain furniture, such as tables and chairs, used for private social gatherings and for playing domino games with friends. It is also not uncommon for parcelas to be decorated with personal touches that reflect the individual tastes, history, and identity of the caretaker. Thus, in Pedro's garden one finds, hanging among the vegetables pieces of colored glass, discarded toys, and other artifacts of personal significance (e.g., a teacup given to him by his last lover). In this sense, parcelas become sites for the display of individual or family identities, intertwined with acts of homemaking and ultimately experienced as private spaces consciously marked off from the world without.[7]

The Garden as Personal Refuge

By the time I met Pedro, his garden had been photographed numerous times by representatives of governmental and nongovernmental institutions and by curious foreigners like me interested in Havana's urban agriculture sites. As he proudly told me, his garden had even been featured on a television program so that strangers now greeted him on the street as "the squash man"—a nickname that alluded to one of the most characteristic features of his garden: the vertical cultivation of squash (see Figure 3.6). In spite of this relative fame, Pedro's garden remained an unseen and unknown space for most people, except for a few institutional visitors, his immediate neighbors, and his close friends. This relative invisibility was fine with Pedro since he valued his privacy.

I met Pedro in 1998 but became close to him later, during my doctoral fieldwork, when I spent many afternoons or mornings in his cramped residence debating all sorts of topics, from Latin American politics to gardening. I knew Pedro had a few friends he occasionally

Figure 3.6. Pedro's garden in full season.

visited, but for the most part he spent his days alone in his three-room home, engrossed in creating paintings using recycled materials. We usually sat close to his drafting table in his bedroom studio (his kitchen resembled a corridor with standing room only, his small dining room was full of boxes, and piles of books and papers were everywhere, including on the table and chairs). Except for a few playful portraits of himself in his garden (see Figure 3.7), which hung in his living room by the entrance door, the rest of his works, while also brightly colored, were filled with skeletons and portrayed a gloomy vision of the world and the future (see Figure 3.8). I knew from our conversations that Pedro had recently experienced the painful end of a relationship and that he felt generally disenchanted with the revolutionary process in which he had once enthusiastically participated. Both factors seemed to have contributed to his bouts of depression in recent years. It seemed as though he had lost hope and had decided to cut himself off from the world.

As I talked to Pedro about his daily life, it became evident that, along with his art, the garden had facilitated this personal separation from the surrounding world. In particular, his vertical cultivation plan not only provided a "hiding place" from the harsh reality without but also allowed

Figure 3.7. Pedro's self-portrait in garden.

him to create a restful space for himself—a space that he connected to an idealized past, when he was hopeful of a better future.

Pedro first described his vertical cultivation plan, which imitated "a forest-like environment," by emphasizing its practicality. The design, which incorporated several levels of crops, not only allowed him to work in a place that was not initially well suited for agricultural production but also maximized the productive capacity of his eight-meter-square parcela. The inspiration for his "tropical forest" design, as he called it, was derived neither from a recent permaculture workshop offered by the FANJNH nor from his prior agricultural experiences in Cuba.[8] Instead, Pedro traced his practices back to a small village in Ukraine that he had visited as a young man while on a scholarship to study engineering in the Soviet Union. Despite the years that had passed, he vividly remembered this rural Ukrainian village, where every house had its own vegetable garden plot and where he had seen "the most beautiful garden one could ever imagine," cultivated by the principal of the local secondary

Figure 3.8. Pedro's rendition of his neighborhood bar.

school. He recounted: "That was a real beauty! I had never seen anything like it. It was intensive cultivation on three levels. On the ground level he had vegetables that needed shade. On the third level he had grapes, melons. On the other level he had potatoes, beets, tomatoes, cucumbers. The school principal told me that with that little lot he sustained himself all year round!" It was not just the productive potential of the garden but also its therapeutic powers that had impressed Pedro. He explained: "That was the first time in my life I heard it said that plants were sensitive, that they were grateful and knew who looked after them, that they emitted a smell imperceptible to our consciousness but which nevertheless is responsible for our sense of well-being in a garden. That school principal told me how the garden served him as entertainment and as a break from problems at the school." Indeed, this role of the garden as a "refuge" from daily problems and grueling routines seemed vital to Pedro, who spent time in his lot not only tending to his plants but also meditating.

Under the squash plants, in an area of the garden so enclosed by vegetation that it allowed for the presence of only a squatting person, Pedro had placed a small stool. It was there, he told me, that he went when he needed to relax. He insisted that I try out the spot, but he first explained what it meant to him and how I should experience it:

> Of course, if you look at this spot from your normal height, you see nothing. It is like trying to see the Amazon from a plane: you see nothing, just a green mass. You have to get into the forest, with the Indians, so to speak, in order to experience the fear of the anacondas and the beauty to be found in the forest. When I sit in my garden in that particular spot, on a small stool, close to the ground, I really feel I am in the middle of the forest and away from everything!

In that spot within his garden Pedro felt he could commune with nature, as if in a forest, away from the world. He could relax because he felt distant from worldly turmoil, and because he had made himself invisible to the world by hiding himself in his "tropical forest."

Pedro was not alone in experiencing his garden as a "refuge." Gabriela, his sixty-eight-year-old next-door neighbor and her seventy-five-year-old husband, Fulgencio, who for years had cultivated vegetables and raised chickens in the lot next to Pedro's, spoke similarly about their garden. After telling me that she would often break into song or poetry while in her garden, Gabriela explained: "I feel happy there, it is a field of peace. . . . As I told you, I find nature wonderful." Fulgencio, for his part, told me: "I find much entertainment, exercise, and breathing space [in the garden]. There I spend the most restful times of my day." Considering that this couple, much like Pedro, experienced their surrounding neighborhood as a hostile place, characterized by noise, social disorder, and a decaying physical environment, it seems that their feeling of relaxation while in the garden derived not only from contact with nature; just as important was the feeling that they had created a separate place of beauty, solace, and tranquil isolation from a world they felt increasingly excluded them. This experience they also shared with another group of nearby neighbors, who attended a daytime clinic for the elderly in the municipality of El Cerro.

This group of elderly people had been working a garden lot that the clinic had created as part of its depression therapy regime, following a FANJNH permaculture workshop offered to patients. Those who participated in the garden had first been drawn to the clinic by a range of circumstances, including the death of a loved one and their inability to cope with an unstable world at a time in their lives when they needed serenity and stability. Although these people participated in other activities at the clinic, they spent most of their time working or contemplating the parcela they cultivated with the assistance of Rafael, a permaculture enthusiast, also from the municipality of El Cerro, who was temporarily hired by the clinic to assist the group in their gardening endeavors.

There were about five patients committed to the garden. Among them was Ramiro, a man in his early seventies who was named a "garden activist" for his enthusiastic participation in the project. He and other participants recounted to me how the garden had reinvigorated their desire to live by connecting them with nature and, importantly, to each other.

During a conversation with Ramiro, I mentioned having seen him on a television program. His eyes lit up with pride as he repeated the sentiments he had expressed during that interview regarding his work at the garden: "I told her [the journalist]: Nobody puts a gun to my head to tell me to come here every morning. I come of my own accord. Could I charge money for this work? Never! I would be a mercenary if I charged for this, after all the help I received. And I am not a mercenary, not even in my most private of thoughts." Volunteering in the garden "free of charge" meant a lot to this group of elderly people who, like Pedro, regretted what they described as the recent *metalización* (slang for commodification) of life in Cuba, where everything, including love, now appeared to be up for sale in a hard-currency economy that alienated and excluded them. For them, the garden was not about money, or f creating a private place for reflection. Instead, it was about the nealing power of the group and the possibility of people having the compassion to care for each other in difficult times. This sentiment was nicely captured in their unanimous decision to plant a bed of spinach in the shape of a heart. While they took produce and herbs from the garden home to share with their families, they were especially proud of the contributions the garden made to the clinic, providing it with herbs and condiments to make meals and herbal infusions for patients like themselves.

As I spent many afternoons and mornings with them, I could not help but think that in their intentions and actions they far surpassed Fuster's expectation of a mere balance among "brain, heart, and pocket." What mattered most for these elderly gardeners, at the end of their life, was friendship and the hope of recuperating a sense of belonging to a caring community. For them, the garden offered solace not in solitude but in company.

Clearly, the impulse of Pedro and his immediate neighbors to cut themselves off from the rest of society was not universal among producers, many of whom saw connection rather than detachment as necessary and desirable. This was the case regarding not just the broader community but also the state and its official programs. While some producers were all too happy to remain distant from state institutions, others sought to connect their garden more closely with the state.

Seeking Recognition in a Fast-Changing World

At the turn of the twenty-first century, some parts of Havana, particularly municipalities frequented by tourists, like La Habana Vieja, appeared to be veritable construction sites, with new hotels, restaurants, and even residences being renovated or constructed at amazing speed with the help of foreign capital. Just a decade earlier, in the same municipalities, gardens had been created by average citizens working with meager resources on many vacant lots where planned construction had been halted because of the state's lack of financial capital (see Figure 3.9).

Figure 3.9. Vacant lot in Centro Habana
after conversion to agriculture.

As already mentioned, these parcelas, as well as the productive patios that were created around the same time and since then, in private court-yards, corridors, and rooftops throughout the city, were much celebrated at the beginning of the Special Period, yet over time they appeared to have fallen off the list of official government priorities. By 2000, most patio and parcela producers in core municipalities felt that their efforts,

while recognized and celebrated by some NGOs and for
had become invisible, even irrelevant, to state actors. This
the perception of Ina, an elderly woman who, along with c
women from her barrio, had been tending a garden on state   ... the
central municipality of Centro Habana. The garden had been started
with the guidance and mediation of an Australian named Liz who lived
in the area and was then in Cuba working for the Australian Conservation Foundation (ACF), assisting the FANJNH with their permaculture
program. The resulting garden was admired by many in the vicinity and
was even included as one of the featured stops in the FANJNH's tour of
model gardens at the end of its permaculture courses. Given this relative fame, Ina was outraged when, upon attending a government meeting in 2001, she found out that the government appeared to be unaware
of the site's existence. At the meeting, officials had been discussing the
upcoming national gathering of parcelas and patios at which model city
gardeners would receive a certificate in recognition of their efforts. When
one of the officials in attendance made a remark about how vegetable
gardens were nonexistent in places like Centro Habana, Ina could not
restrain herself. She told me she not only publicly corrected the misin-
formed official but also told him that he might as well start preparing
the certificate of recognition for her garden since it was one of the few
and the most impressive in the municipality. As she told me the story she
added indignantly, "Imagine, they don't even know my garden exists!"[9]
An active member of her CDR and a self-declared revolutionary herself, Ina felt that it was not a good thing for these small-scale gardens to
have fallen below the radar of the state and to have suffered such relative
neglect. As she talked about this incident, her experience of having been
overlooked by the pertinent level of government in this enterprise resonated with other stories of similar feelings of disconnection, abandon-
ment, and neglect experienced by the broader population at the time.

In the end, Ina succeeded in getting the attention of the pertinent
state officials. She was personally invited to attend the First Annual
National Meeting of the Patio and Parcela Movement, where her garden was awarded the title of model garden for her municipality, and she
even received a small prize—a shovel—for her accomplishments. She

was pleased with this recognition, as were many other gardeners who attended this meeting and other, similar gatherings.

From a certain perspective that holds at bay the visions and plans of decision makers and focuses instead on the personal dimensions of patios and parcelas for those who inhabit these spaces, urban agriculture appears to be less about consciously struggling to save *la revolución*, as some officials claim, than about personal survival in a context of scarcity; less about a well-integrated community than about the marginalization of certain sectors of the population and their attempts at reconnecting to each other and the broader society. Public recognition of their achievements seemed to be a special source of pride for many of the producers.

While marginal in relation to the most dynamic sectors of the Cuban economy and suffering from relative neglect from official state actors, parcelas and patios and their associated producers do not represent autonomous spaces and actors that can (or necessarily want to) exist independently from the sociopolitical context in which they are embedded. Even in cases like that of Pedro and some of his neighbors, who expressed a desire to disconnect, total disconnection and autonomy from "the world outside" are neither a possibility nor something deemed ideal.

As the next chapter will illustrate, patios and parcelas—like other similarly marginalized spaces—are grounds that breed debate and reflection about recent and prior government policies in a way that directly connects to ongoing debates in society at large. Dwelling in these spaces entails, at a minimum, reflecting on the ideal organization and use of space and on who should have ultimate authority over it. It further encourages reflection on questions pertaining to food production and food provisioning in Cuba. These reflections, in turn, underscore the changing sensibilities of a population that has become increasingly aware of the flaws of previous models of development (and governance) in Cuba and is ready to voice its opinion on what might constitute a better alternative for the country and even for the survival of *la revolución*.

4

Claiming Space,
Questioning the Order of Things

In early 2001, I attended an official meeting that was called to discuss the integration of urban agriculture into the master plan of Havana. Many institutional actors involved in urban planning were in attendance. Also at the meeting were a few parceleros invited to give their opinion as practitioners. Among the latter was Benancio, an affable retired army man who, along with other ex-FAR members, had been cultivating a parcela in the municipality of Habana del Este.

The meeting began with the professionals in the room giving their opinion on how to better control and regulate agriculture in the city. People from the GDIC said that planners needed to engage the community in the planning process—a comment supported by Benancio, who interjected:

> I think it is fundamental to give power to the individual inhabitant as the creator of space. Martí said it a long time ago: "With everyone and for the benefit of everyone."[1] I think it is the same story here. Sometimes, we want to build a town and a single person decides where the streets will go, and later, when people try to use the streets, they do not find their location convenient. When I started working for the Revolutionary Armed Forces, a comrade told me that when he had to set up a camp, he would first place the services and would only draw the paths once people showed him, through use, where the best place for them would be. And so I want to say

that no architect, no civil engineer can ever substitute the capacity of the average individual to solve the problems she or he faces.

He insisted: "When we want to succeed at something, let's give real participation to the masses, and they will find the best solutions. . . . No learned knowledge can substitute for lived experience. Practical knowledge is superior to any knowledge a man seated behind a desk can ever attain."

Benancio's plea to hand over decision-making power to "the masses" was very much in tune with "the revolutionary spirit," and even coincided with the GDIC's mandate of participatory planning. Yet his words made those present uneasy, as many of them fit the description of state functionaries who, indeed, spent most of their time behind a desk, far removed from the daily experiences of those directly engaged in the practice of urban agriculture in Havana.

Like the activities organized by the first horticulturalist clubs in Santa Fé, Benancio's interventions at this meeting were not intended to attack or undermine the broader project associated with *la revolución* but rather to point to the detrimental effects of inadequate community participation and the not always wise choice, on the part of the government, to rely on the opinions of experts whose knowledge was presumed to be superior to that of the common man or woman. As Benancio suggested, these experts might do better if they learned to incorporate the wisdom and actual practices of city inhabitants into their urban planning designs. Sentiments like these were frequently expressed by urban agriculture practitioners whose experiences in this field had given them ample opportunity to reflect on the ways space, food production, and food distribution were currently organized in Cuba.

This chapter outlines how involvement in urban agriculture encourages critical reflection on established state practices and fosters feelings of competence and independence among producers who now feel entitled to have an opinion on agricultural and urban matters and resent unwanted government interference in their affairs. As will be addressed in the last section of the chapter, the relative independence

it, fenced it in properly, and so on. Well, it would seem that our plight was understood in higher spheres and they [the architects] have not returned to bother us since.

While acknowledging the help they received from local government representatives who assisted by lending them tools—such as a wheelbarrow—and by arranging for a truck to pick up the bulk of the rubble, all the gardeners on Dawn Street underscored their own personal efforts to clean and prepare the lot for cultivation. Clearing the place of debris, and later filling each lot (which still contained the demolished building foundations) with soil to prepare it for gardening, was mentioned as the most arduous work. Pedro explained: "[The gardens] had to be made from scratch; the soil had to be brought in by wheelbarrow. Each person worked his own lot." He repeated:

The ground had to be constructed from scratch. I had a wife then and she helped me. We tore down part of the wall together and I worked from seven in the morning until nine in the evening bringing in soil. I brought the soil in sacks on a bike! And we did it. It was madness because I had to bring seventy sacks of soil! Then the local government representative gave me a wheelbarrow and on it I brought two sacks at a time. It was a huge wheelbarrow yet the sacks barely fit. I brought them from far away, from a place where the soil was not being used. I had to go up an enormous hill; it was hard work!

Most parceleros equally underscored the individual physical efforts and personal investment involved in clearing and preparing usufruct lots, characterizing these activities as acts of *saneamiento* (sanitization) of places that, left to the community at a time when the state was unable to exert control over them, had become sites for disease breeding and social disorder (see Figure 4.2).[5] Pedro tellingly ended his account by saying, "Nobody else would bother preparing and cleaning the site under those conditions." This alone, he felt, had entitled him and the others to the site, giving them an almost inalienable right to it. He told me, "Who

Figure 4.2. Recuperated lot in the municipality of Plaza.

is going to take this away from me after all the work I have done on it?" Commenting specifically on the incident with the architects, he added: "That cannot be taken away. How could those who gave it to us take it away? Why would the government take it away when it was under agricultural production and there were other lots bette construction?"

Such assertions of private entitlement to vacant state lots ﹀ mon among parceleros who often questioned the official p..erence for this land to be centrally managed; its use defined, at a distance, by experts in urban planning. The overall consensus among parceleros appeared to be that private citizens, rather than state employees, knew best and had proven themselves to be the ideal caretakers of public land. This underlying critique of state control and management extended also to producers' assessment of the state's involvement in food production.

Growing One's Own Food, Reflecting on State Inefficiencies

Implicit in the narratives of many of the producers I interviewed was a criticism of the state's inability to properly provide for the food needs of the population. This expression of disapproval often linked up with negative reflections on the centralized, large-scale organization of the socialist economy and the poor quality of resulting products. Although these criticisms had been circulating in the broader society for quite some time, they especially resonated with the experiences of patio and parcela owners.

Personal experience in food production, when successful, led producers to question the supposed superiority of state-managed agriculture. They often spoke about how their products compared favorably with those acquired through the state system. Pedro, for example, went on at length about the size of the produce he had grown on his small lot, which included habanero peppers the size of an egg, regular peppers that weighed five pounds each, and string beans thirty inches long! These, he mentioned, were things he had never seen in his life. Along similar lines, Rafael, another producer also from the municipality of El Cerro, remarked about the "abysmal" difference in the size and quality of the plantains he grew at home and those he would purchase at the state food stalls (see Figure 4.3). "It is the technique I use," he explained, "because I

Figure 4.3. Garden in Habana del Este with plantains
and part of a wooden beehive to the right.

give them personal care." Manolo bragged about how his rabbits grew at
a rate that far exceeded the state average: "At forty-five days, they already
weigh from two and a half to three pounds. One only hears about such
growth in books that talk about rabbits in France, Italy, Spain. Yet, I
do it here at home with my homemade feed, without getting help from
anyone." The implication in each case was that the products grown by
individual small-scale producers were better because they were given
individual care; they were not mass produced like those provided by the
state.

It was not just the size and overall quality of the resulting produce or
meat that were commented on but also its freshness. For Roberto, the

freshness and taste of the rabbits he raised on his rooftop were a huge reward for his labor. He told me, "It is not the same to eat a fresh rabbit as to eat one that has been in the freezer for a while." Again, drawing a negative comparison with state-produced meat, he added: "The pork that they sell to us at the market has been previously frozen; that pork could have been dead for ten years for all we know. One cannot compare that to a freshly slaughtered pig that has been raised at home."

In this manner, producers' discussion of their products often connected with an implicit or explicit negative evaluation of state-centralized, large-scale agriculture and food distribution systems run by state workers with little personal investment or pride in their work. Some of these criticisms paralleled public government debates on the inefficiencies of agricultural production and the need for adequate remuneration of workers in this sector. Despite this convergence in critiques, however, there were important differences between the opinions expressed by a majority of state officials at this time and those of small-scale producers. For example, in official circles private, small-scale agricultural production was still presented not as the ideal but rather as a necessary response to exceptional conditions.[6] By contrast, from the perspective of parceleros and patio owners, this form of production, while triggered by necessity, was unequivocally the superior choice, at least in terms of the quality and taste of resulting products.

In addition to allowing producers the enjoyment of better-quality food, urban agriculture freed them from the vagaries of state food supplies. This earned independence was a source of pride for many producers who often felt they had an advantage over many of their neighbors in this respect and were glad that, at least for the time being, they were able to help themselves with the official endorsement of a government that previously had condemned the pursuit of purely individual (as opposed to communal) self-sufficiency.

Tasting Independence:
Resenting Uncertainty and Control

The move from a situation where citizens were told they could expect "everything from the state" to one where they were encouraged to help themselves through their own means and labor could have, as was the case with many nonurban farmers I knew, triggered a condemnation of the state as defaulting on its obligations to the population.[7] This, however, was not the case with the producers I knew, who tended to focus on the positive dimension of this shift. Rather than frame the experience as a loss of rights as citizens of the Cuban nation, the producers I worked with felt they had gained the ability to better cope with the chronic food scarcity that, albeit in less pronounced forms, had existed at other times since the 1959 revolution (see Figures 4.4 and 4.5). Roberto, describing his rooftop rabbit production, told me, "I raise these animals because, basically, when meat is scarce, I can kill one of my animals and have food for my family." Along the same lines, Román, talking about his parcela, explained: "Look, now my hen is roosting and I have three eggs guaranteed. Eggs have not come through the ration in a while, but I have my eggs. While others don't have any, I have mine. Why? Because I raise chickens in my lot."

This relative independence from the vagaries of state provisions was much appreciated by producers who, nevertheless, felt (and often resented) that their ability to engage in urban agriculture was itself dependent on the goodwill of state institutions that had the power to shut down their production for a number of reasons. Parceleros worried about the possibility of suddenly losing their usufruct rights to higher-priority functions. Those involved in animal breeding felt particularly vulnerable to accusations of engaging in black market trade (many used illegally purchased industrial feed) or of posing a health risk to the population through unhygienic practices and keeping animals with potentially transferable diseases.

Even when producers understood that the state had the right to intervene in these areas, official interference in individual production endeavors was usually resented and presented as erratic and irrational,

Figure 4.4. Goats for meat and milk.

Figure 4.5. More than enough herbs to share.

influenced more by political agendas and personal pettiness than by legitimate concerns. Manolo recounted how, years prior, before the Special Period, public health officials had made him slaughter all the chickens he was raising at home because a neighbor had complained about a bad smell attributed to a lack of hygiene. He commented, laughing, that the smell that probably bothered his neighbor was that of fried chicken he could not eat. With the intention of pointing out the inconsistencies in the actions of state representatives (and by extension of the state itself), he continued: "Now, as you can see, I am raising rabbits in the same or worse conditions, yet they [state functionaries] applaud my work. It is as happened with John Lennon. When I was young they put me in jail because they found me with a Beatles record. Now, our commander-in-chief [Fidel] sits beside [the newly installed] John Lennon statue and poses for the camera with his arm around him as if they were good friends!"[8]

Roberto, who at the time had become quite close to Manolo through their shared interest in rabbit breeding, made a similar point in a separate conversation:

You came in '97, and then in 2001, right? Perhaps you will return in 2005 and you'll find we still have rabbits. But then again, perhaps it will be all over by then. There is nothing fixed or constant here. They [those in government] may get up one morning and tell you that you cannot raise rabbits anymore because they are bad for the birds or whatever, and you have to get rid of them. . . . It is not like other places where things are stable. No, here someone [in government] could say tomorrow that agriculture is not a good idea anymore, that now we need to search for petroleum, and the following day everyone would be digging holes in the ground. The next day, the directive can change again: "Now we need to go to the moon" and everyone goes to the moon. Years ago, I could not have a conversation with a foreigner. Now, it is OK for me to be talking to you. This isn't easy, girl!

Indeed, by 2005, Roberto had stopped his rabbit breeding because he was finding it nearly impossible to find adequate feed for his animals. The irony of the government promoting the raising of rabbits for household self-provisioning without at the same time ensuring the easy availability of feed was not lost on Roberto.

Both producers turned their commentaries about the instability of their urban agriculture endeavors into a broader criticism of what they understood to be the general modus operandi of the government, which they characterized as whimsical, irrational, and prone to drastic reversals.[9] Their explicit complaint only underscored the overall feeling of many producers who, despite their current relative independence in production, recognized that the state still held the ultimate trump card over their lives and their livelihoods, even when, as will be explained shortly, as producers they also held considerable power over lower-ranking employees of institutions like the MINAG.

In this context, producers did not take anything for granted but remained ready for the rules of the game to change at any time, scheming to stay always one step ahead of government prohibitions or contrary orders. Manolo told me: "The day they prohibit rabbits, I will start raising smaller animals. And let them beware because there will come a time when I will be raising ants or mosquitoes at home, and they will be the biggest specimens of each ever seen [*laughs*]. Imagine the biggest mosquito and the biggest ant!" Despite the playfulness of this statement, the message was clear: producers would comply on the surface, but they would not totally give up on doing what they wanted or needed to do to survive.

Producers found fault not just with government policies and actions but also with government inaction. Connecting with Roberto's concern over the poor availability of feed, Manolo complained that if the government were serious about solving "the protein problem" for the population, it would set up animal feed production centers in every municipality, using as a model his homemade dehydrator of kitchen leftovers. He had mentioned this idea to the MINAG representatives and the delegate of agriculture, who had visited him several times. He had even offered his expertise and assistance, yet, although they seemed to admire his work, they never took him up on his offer. He commented:

> The feed could then be sold cheaply to producers while one transformed garbage [kitchen scraps] into meat. Oh, but no, nobody listens to me! Nobody comes and says, "Come and tell my boss your idea." . . . I can assure you that Fidel is sufficiently intelligent that if he were to see this, he would come out of this house and say, "Don't let this old guy get away until he gets this project done." Come on! This country has seen such harebrained ideas carried out, wilder dreams that never amounted to anything, but this idea has "swing," it makes sense.

Regardless of whether Manolo was right in thinking his animal feed scheme would be easy for the government to implement on a large scale at the municipal level, what is important to note is that what bothered him was the fact that his opinion, experience, and expertise in this area were not taken into account by those state representatives in charge of urban agriculture. In this respect, his commentary resonated with Benancio's words, cited at the beginning of this chapter, which called for greater input, participation, and consultation of those who, day after day, faced the challenges of engaging in primary food production in Havana.

Somewhat contradicting these producers' perceptions that their knowledge was not considered important by decision makers, there were indications that the MINAG at this time was indeed interested in learning about producers' creative solutions to common production problems.[10] Adolfito, the national president of the Urban Agriculture Department, made this quite clear at the 2001 First Annual National Meeting of the Patio and Parcela Movement. Then, as he described the gardens he visited prior to the meeting, he commented, as cited in Chapter 1, on how he had seen "things that show the wisdom, innovativeness, and intelligence of our people." He added:

> It is crucial that these initiatives be recorded by province, by CDR. . . . For instance, the innovation of manual [agricultural] implements should be communicated upward; it should be brought to our attention, with a sketch and a brief description attached, because we are lagging behind here and there are great inventions that remain to be discovered. . . . All sorts of things have been invented in Cuba, but we have not been able to find a way to network and disseminate these ideas.

The "discovery" of such inventions, as well as their dissemination and implementation on a large scale, as suggested by Adolfito, required not only well-trained staff attuned to what might be worth "communicating upward" but also resources that the MINAG simply did not have. In addition, it was clear that such inventions could be procured only if "the inventors" themselves were as willing to share their knowledge as Manolo seemed to be.

New Modes of Governance: Turning Power Around?

By 2002, official statistics reported a total 104,087 patios and parcelas, covering an area of approximately 3,595 hectares spread throughout various Havana municipalities. To oversee these sites, the MINAG had assigned one delegate of agriculture per municipality who was assisted by a number of agriculture representatives usually in charge of two districts each.

The delegate of agriculture had a number of duties, including ensuring that Agricultural Input Stores were well stocked and that larger-scale production sites, like organopónicos, made timely deliveries to schools and hospitals. Although the delegates received material incentives for their work (e.g., they got a percentage of all contracts negotiated by Agricultural Input Stores), their responsibilities were too varied, their territories too vast, and their available material resources too meager for them to be able to adequately fulfill their multiple roles. Regla, the delegate for the municipality of El Cerro, whom I first met in 1997, did her job for years without having access to her own vehicle. It was only in 2001, after seven years in the same position, that the government was able to give her a brand-new motorcycle to facilitate covering her assigned territory. She was thrilled, but while the motorcycle no doubt made her job easier, it did not necessarily translate into her making more frequent visits to the parceleros and patio owners in her municipality who complained she visited only once a year and then only if they had been selected as model gardeners.

The agriculture representatives were more likely to visit small-scale producers since their only job was to cater to them, yet they had fewer material resources at their disposal than the delegates did and, for most of them, transportation was a problem. Ihosvany, a MINAG representative who had two districts under his care in El Cerro, for example, got around on foot, on an old bike, or by unreliable public transportation. He had to travel every day from his home in Centro Habana to his office at the CDR headquarters in El Cerro. His office, in turn, was more than thirty blocks from his assigned districts. He told me he felt bad that he could not reach everyone in his territory, but there was little else he could do given the circumstances.

Despite the fact that his MINAG salary was very modest, Ihosvany took his job seriously and tried hard to meet his duties. By the time I met him in 2001, he had been on the job for only eight months, yet he was clearly worn down by the demands placed on him. Because he had been hired after the launching of the Patio and Parcela Movement, one of the jobs he was expected to do was to recruit as many gardeners as possible into the movement. On top of this, he had to provide the municipal delegate with the statistics needed for the trimonthly reports on the progress of urban agriculture in the territory, which would later be used to produce the global statistics used in MINAG reports.

I came to know Ihosvany and Raquel, a MINAG representative for Centro Habana, quite well and on several occasions accompanied them on their job rounds. From our many conversations, I learned that they felt they had little to offer producers, yet depended on their goodwill to get their job done. On the one hand, they needed to persuade individual citizens to convert their private patios, rooftops, and balconies into productive gardens, thereby enhancing MINAG statistics in the area. On the other, they needed to recruit existing producers already working from patios or parcelas to participate in MINAG programs, such as the national competition for the title of model garden, intended to guide the development of these sites. The accounts by Ihosvany, Raquel, and other MINAG employees clearly indicated that when it came to parcelas and patios, voluntary involvement in government programs, rather than enforcement through coercive mechanisms, was thought to be the best (and only) path of action.

Talking about patios, Raquel explained that given the "weak nature of state influence and authority" over these spaces, her work had to be carried out "without violating individual will." Regla, the delegate of El Cerro, echoed this sentiment as she told me, "Of course, our work with patios is difficult because we cannot just show up and tell the owner, 'Look, you have to do this.'" A member of the Provincial Urban Agriculture Department for Havana elaborated in another conversation: "A patio is different from an organopónico. The patio has to be considered from the perspective that it is the producer's. We can give advice and lend support to the producer *but we cannot demand* anything from him nor expect that he sow what we tell him to" (emphasis hers). These and other statements I collected illustrated how MINAG employees recognized that small-scale producers had a fair degree of independence. Unless producers were engaging in illegal activities, MINAG employees could not tell patio owners, or parceleros for that matter, what to do on their site. Compared to members of other organizations, whose work was not only less constrained by government bureaucracy but greatly facilitated by more direct access to international funding or tourism revenues, MINAG staff like Ihosvany and Raquel had little to offer small-scale producers when it came to concrete resources and training. This situation, however, did not mean that state institutions, like the MINAG, with official jurisdiction over urban agriculture, had lost their power over the relevant population. In fact, as will be seen in the next two chapters, as the overall raison d'être of parcelas and patios changed and new institutional actors appeared to compete for producers' loyalties, state institutions like the MINAG, the urban planning office, and the local government continued to exert remarkable influence over producers, even at a distance.

5

State Land, Green Agendas, Old Ideas, and Community Work

In September 2001, as part of a sustainable agriculture course offered by the FANJNH, I joined a group of Cubans on a tour of city gardens. The tour was meant to provide participants with inspiration for a final course assignment: the design of a permaculture-inspired garden that, following the teachings of Australians Bill Mollison and David Holmgren, would create a closed production system that would mimic "nature" in form and function. Among the gardens we visited, there was one I had seen months earlier as I accompanied a Cuba solidarity brigade from England interested in learning from and volunteering with Havana's urban farmers under the guidance of the FANJNH.

This garden was located on state land in an outlying district in the touristic municipality of Habana Vieja. With its neat rows of rectangular cultivation beds of one crop each, it hardly met the permaculture standards of intercropping and curvilinear design.[1] What the site lacked in design appeal, however, it made up for in suitability for large-group visits. Measuring about twenty-five by eleven meters in size, it was roomy enough to allow many people to be on site at the same time. Moreover, the garden excelled in terms of hospitality. Its caretaker was an affable septuagenarian named Jorge whose home terrace, one level up at the back of the garden, could comfortably hold about twenty people for a feast that Jorge's wife, María, willingly prepared for a reasonable fee. Given all of this, it was no surprise that the garden was a favorite stop for the FANJNH tours.

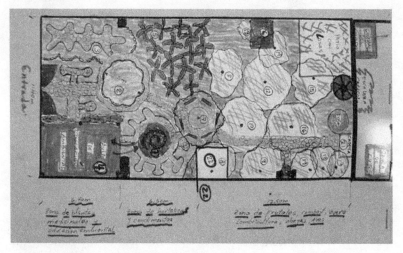

**Figure 5.1. Planned permaculture design for Jorge's parcela
(terrace to the right).**

Over the years, I got to know Jorge and María independently of the
foundation. I visited them often and even lived with them for a short
time. One afternoon, as we sat on their home terrace, Jorge talked about
his aspirations for the garden. He told me about how, after taking his
first permaculture design course with the FANJNH, he had started
thinking about how to make the garden more sustainable and aestheti-
cally pleasing. As he spoke about this, María, ran into the house and
brought back the design he and a colleague had drawn up after completing the FANJNH course (see Figure 5.1). When I commented on how
little this design resembled the current appearance of the garden, Jorge
explained that he could not single-handedly bring this new plan to frui-
tion with his meager material resources. "That little piece of land is my
dream," he said. "I would love for people walking by to stop and say,
'Look how beautiful that garden looks,' but I lack the resources. I only
earn ninety-four pesos and I cannot take from my salary to buy things
for the garden."

Things like hoses, a water pump, and other materials needed to build a planned fish pond and a staircase that would connect the terrace of his home with the garden below were expensive. The ladder alone would cost fifteen hundred pesos, an impossible proposition for a man whose retirement salary was under one hundred pesos a month. As María explained, Jorge could not even afford to buy the variety of fruit trees and medicinal herbs that would move the garden closer to the biodiversity ideal promoted by the FANJNH. The foundation had provided Jorge with some necessary agricultural inputs (e.g., it had arranged for the delivery of a couple truckloads of topsoil), but this assistance was insufficient.

To complicate things further, Jorge's parcela had recently come under threat of "eviction," and he now felt that improving the site was pointless, unless he could ensure the government's continued support. In the early 1990s, a government representative had granted authorization (though not in writing) for the cultivation of the site, but things had changed since that time: the economy was doing much better, vegetables were more readily accessible to the population at large, and major state investment in construction was once again possible, especially in touristic districts like Habana Vieja. These changes made it difficult to defend the continued permanence of parcelas like Jorge's that had come into existence at a time when the state had few resources for urban development and food insecurity was high. Yet, as will be shown, parcelas were defended by a range of institutions which needed these sites in order to carry out new projects of their own.

This chapter considers how the survival of parcelas that were not particularly successful in terms of output came to rest primarily on the arguments that could be made regarding their contribution to the community in social and environmental terms.[2] The chapter explores how this emphasis on community and the environment represents an important shift in the meaning attributed to these sites—a shift that while connecting with old state projects also points to new state and nonstate projects that encourage citizens to take responsibility not just for themselves and their families but for the community as a whole, engaging them in volunteer activities such as environmental education "in and for the neighborhood."

In particular, the case analyzed here illustrates how parceleros try—not always successfully—to balance multiple institutional expectations with their own personal projects, which include retaining custody over their sites. The case serves to show how values traditionally associated with the revolutionary project continue to exert their influence over the population "conducting the conduct" of individuals imperceptibly, without the need for overt rules or constant coercion from those in positions of authority (Foucault 1980, 1991; Dean 1999). Indeed, what becomes evident in this case (and the one described in Chapter 6) is the extent to which "average" citizens are engaged in reasserting values that uphold a communitarian outlook in a context where recent government policies and actions appear to be moving in the opposite direction. This exposition further reveals how ideas associated with a communitarian ethos are deployed with very different intentions and effects by differently situated actors. In this respect, the analysis suggests that state projects and ideologies in Cuba, as elsewhere, not only allow for alternative readings and enactments but also, being far from all-encompassing, always leave room for counterhegemonic projects to flourish. These alternative projects, as Tania Li (2005, 2007) has pointed out in reference to World Bank–funded projects in Indonesia, do not exist "outside of power." They are autonomous from neither the state nor from state-like institutions, such as national NGOs and transnational organizations, which are equally invested in influencing the conduct of the population.

Tourist Dollars, Foreign Connections, and Opportune Collaborations

One afternoon, as we sipped his acidic homemade wine sitting under the mature grapevine on his home terrace, Jorge told me: "I often sit under it [the vine] and dream about all the things I would like to do in the garden. I wish things were more certain, that I could plan what I want to do there. True, the site was given to me by the president of the Poder Popular, but I have nothing that says 'this is yours' or that 'it is for everyone's benefit.' Someone could come tomorrow, after all I've done there, and say, 'You have to fell that tree' or 'Pull everything out of there.'" He lamented, "I say the garden is mine because this guy gave it to me, but I cannot really say that it is truly mine."

This acute awareness that the place was not "truly his" was connected to the already-mentioned threat of eviction, which had originated in part from a relatively new neighborhood institution, created in 1994, known as the Taller de Renovación de Barrio (Neighborhood Revitalization Workshop; henceforth Taller).[3] Since the Taller at the time appeared to have more decision-making power at the district level than the office of the elected municipal government, or Poder Popular, which Jorge had previously dealt with, this was no small threat.

The Taller was a dependency of the Office of the Historian of the City, a cultural institution run by Eusebio Leal, the same person who in the early 1990s had initially opposed General Sio Wong's petition to create an organopónico on Fifth Avenue and, allegedly, later praised the general for making lettuce plants look like flowers. Leal had for years been in charge of the architectural restoration of the municipality of Habana Vieja, whose impressive building stock, dating to colonial times, had resulted in its being named a UNESCO heritage site in 1982. With the onset of the Special Period and the rise of tourism as a crucial source of state revenue, Leal's office had rapidly risen in importance so that, by 1994, it was granted a series of special privileges. This office was now in charge of not only managing building renovations but also securing and reinvesting funds derived from international collaborations and tourist-related business activity in the territory. Rather than being encumbered by the prerequisites of various levels of governmental bureaucracy, the Office of the Historian dealt directly with the Council of State. The main objective of these privileges was to allow for the rapid physical, economic, social, and cultural revitalization of Habana Vieja—something that, of course, positively connected with the touristic development of the municipality. Leal, a trusted citizen with an unblemished record in terms of his ethics and disinterested commitment to the renovation project, was seen by many as the man holding the biggest purse in the city. This was reflected even in the way people in other municipalities talked about him. For example, at a winemakers' club meeting in the municipality of Santos Suárez, a partly inebriated Cuban intellectual (not a club member) toasted the amateur winemakers, saying that their product was so good they should commercialize it through the hard-currency stores run by the Office of the Historian in Habana Vieja. He added, "As they say, all roads lead not to Rome but to Leal!" While for the winemakers in question Leal, his resources, and his power were a long distance away, for Jorge the situation was different. Jorge's home and garden fell under the jurisdiction of the Office of the Historian and the Taller.

In 1999, following its mandate of working with the community to identify its needs, the Taller implemented a series of participatory planning workshops. After the community identified the need for green and recreational space in the area, the Taller organized a mapping exercise intended to note available space that could be used to meet those needs.[4] It was at this point that some neighbors voiced the opinion that Jorge's parcela site would better serve the community as a domino playing ground. By then, as a Taller member explained, citizens in the area had realized that land in Havana Vieja was "valuable real estate," and some resented the idea of public land ending up in the hands of a single individual.[5] Besides, the dispute had come to the attention of a government functionary in charge of mapping and controlling the use of vacant lots in the municipality, who, being biased against vegetable gardens in the area, was likely to shut it down.

Before a final decision was made, the Taller hired a young social psychologist named Juliana. Inspired by the ideas of two freelance garden activists, including Rafael, who was then coordinating the garden at the previously mentioned day clinic in El Cerro, Juliana defended the site with the intention of using it as a home base to teach neighborhood schoolchildren the health benefits of consuming vegetables and the value of contact with nature in the city. As she put it later, the Taller "was searching for a link between the environmental needs identified by the community and a real possibility to work on these, from and with the neighborhood." From the broader perspective of the Office of the Historian, endorsing such a garden in Habana Vieja not only served to address one of the identified needs of the resident population but also importantly assuaged domestic and international criticism that the territory's

93

touristic development prioritized revenue-making projects over the needs and well-being of local inhabitants who were, after all, acknowledged to be part of the charm of the municipality.[6] The garden project would have the added value of helping schools in the area meet the recent government directives that they teach children good eating habits and environmental values. Moreover, this objective fit nicely with a new nationwide government campaign, endorsed by Fidel himself, to encourage healthier eating habits among Cubans. There was no doubt that this reframing of the garden made it relevant to current developments beyond anything the domino-game advocates could have dreamed of for their own proposal, and so, after a protracted seven-month dispute, the garden project was approved.

In March 2001, a number of interested citizens founded the Grupo Barrial de Educación Ambiental (Neighborhood Environmental Education Group, GBEA) to coordinate the garden project. In attendance at the first meeting were a number of neighborhood participants, including Jorge, a CDR representative, a retired librarian from a literary circle, two primary school teachers from the area, and the leader of the neighborhood youth dance troupe. The nonresidents in the group included Juliana, a young member of the Cuban Botanical Association, two other garden activists from elsewhere the city, Rafael, and myself.[7] Juliana informed the group that CIERIC (Centro de Intercambio y Referencia sobre Iniciativas Comunitarias, Center for Exchange and Reference for Community Initiatives), an internationally funded Cuban NGO founded in 1991, had just launched a competition for "novel, participatory, and sustainable projects," which might make it possible for the Taller to obtain some financial support for the garden.[8] At the next meeting, in anticipation of this funding, Jorge was asked to list the things he needed. His list included the items he had mentioned to me: a water pump to facilitate irrigation, seedlings, and a metal staircase to connect the site with his terrace so he would not have to walk halfway around the block to access the garden. Other items, such as stools and other materials required to teach the schoolchildren, were added to the list by other group members.

It was probably clear to Jorge at this point that the GBEA needed him for its environmental project to succeed and that, at the same time, his parcela stood to benefit from his involvement in the GBEA. It was probably also obvious that such benefits required certain commitments on his part, such as tending to the planned weekly meetings with school-children. It is my sense, however, that Jorge did not fully anticipate the kinds of demands the group would place on him, not just regarding activities in the parcela but in his own private space.

Enforcing Responsible Citizenship: The Public Spills into the Private

The second meeting of the GBEA took place on April 10, 2001. We all sat around the table on Jorge's terrace in an area that acted as an impro-vised kitchen. The atmosphere at the meeting was very jovial, with much laughter and teasing, particularly after Jorge brought out a bottle of his homemade wine and invited everyone to taste it. Among the topics dis-cussed was the need to include Jorge's garden in the official program for the upcoming neighborhood Spring Festival, organized by the Taller. The idea was that this would give local residents, as well as people from other parts of the city, an opportunity to learn about the garden, encour-aging further involvement and support for the project.

Everyone had suggestions regarding what to highlight. One partici-pant suggested displaying guinea pigs, which were being promoted by the MINAG as a good source of protein and a safe and easy animal for urban dwellers to care for. This commentary prompted Juliana to men-tion how the group should inform itself as to the regulations restricting the raising of food animals in the area. To my surprise, no one men-tioned the animals that were being raised illegally on the very terrace where we were sitting. At its rear, under the grapevine where Jorge often dreamed of his parcela, one could hear, coming from two cement pens, the noises of an enormous pig and the two piglets waiting to replace it upon its demise. He had proudly shown them to me before the meeting. Without my prompting he had explained how he received only ninety-four pesos a month from his pension and that he and his wife could not afford to live on that. With no reliable source of water, the garden was

95

producing very little; he added, "What we need is some protein," and the pigs provided that.

During the harshest years of the Special Period Fidel himself declared an amnesty on pig raising in the city. Yet by early 2002, when the government believed pork was readily available through agricultural markets, Fidel reversed this amnesty by announcing the launching of an official campaign to end pig raising in Havana (Acosta 2002). Despite clear official legislation strictly banning the keeping of pigs in residential urban areas,[9] the local authorities I met often looked the other way. The representative for the MINAG in Centro Habana told me that while the practice "should not be encouraged to develop any further . . . the current low levels can be tolerated." A Ministry of Public Health inspector working in the same area mentioned that she did not have the heart to denounce an old man she knew to be raising a pig on his home patio since this was an important source of food for him.

The pigs on Jorge's terrace appeared to have been likewise ignored by officials and neighbors until he became involved with the environmental group. A few days after the second meeting, as I returned to Jorge's house to take part in the neighborhood Spring Festival celebrations, I found out that Jorge had slaughtered the adult pig and had gotten rid of the two piglets. At first he calmly told me that he had decided instead to raise guinea pigs, which were legal and a good source of protein. Later, after the festival, he confided that he was instructed to get rid of the animals by people from the Taller because his pig raising was illegal and could jeopardize the health of the community. As his wife commented, they could even get a fine from the Ministry of Public Health. Besides, the practice went against the very concept of sustainability promoted by the GBEA, since it was thought that pig manure and urine were neither safe nor easy to compost, only adding to the waste produced in the neighborhood.

The fact that the pig-raising practices of other "independent" producers I knew in the city were ignored while Jorge became the target of disciplinary actions suggested that going public as an urban farmer involved submitting to a process of official scrutiny that extended far beyond the space of the parcela, as borrowed state land, and reached well into the private domain. An aspiring model producer like Jorge had to live up to the highest societal standards.

Jorge's involvement in the project not only curtailed his most "private" agricultural activities but also led to a loss of control over how he spent his time. As the GBEA's project grew, Jorge's life became more and more entangled in a series of commitments, including regular visits from schoolchildren from the four primary schools in the district and impromptu visits from foreigners or nationals interested in the work being done on the parcela.[10] Soon, Jorge lost the kind of independence that many of the urban farmers I worked with valued about the practice, while "the community," embodied in the GBEA, gained more and more control over a space that Jorge had previously been able to use as his own.

Asserting the Primacy of the Community

According to Juliana, one of the objectives of the GBEA was "to transform a site that was initially private—his [Jorge's] and his family's—into a communitarian space that would nurture a healthier relationship between the community and the natural environment." In some respects, this objective paralleled the actions of similar initiatives endorsed by the government, such as the CDR-MINAG model garden competition, which also aimed at reclaiming public spaces that had become too private and separated from the broader community. From the first meeting the group had in March 2001 to the last meeting I attended in July 2002, I had many opportunities to observe how this resocialization of the site was reflected in its changing functions and associated public representations.

During the first few meetings of the GBEA, those in attendance constantly made reference to *el huerto de Jorge* (Jorge's garden), yet beginning with the second meeting, the formal minutes, prepared by Juliana, referred simply to "the garden on such and such a street" or to the *huerto comunitario* (communitarian garden). By August 2001, when funding from CIERIC had already been confirmed for the project and the group

97

began to meet regularly with a funder's representative in attendance, discussion of "the community" and its participation dominated the agenda.

Over time, a number of special neighborhood activities were organized with the stated objective of "getting the residents to perceive the garden as a communitarian garden." Regardless of the relative lack of community participation in these activities, Nancy, a GBEA member in her midfifties who was the leader of the neighborhood literary circle, abruptly asserted at one of the meetings: "The garden is the neighborhood's patio. It's not Jorge's garden. It is a *communitarian* garden" (emphasis hers).

Months later, during the second Spring Festival in May 2002, I encountered Nancy in the Neighborhood Community House, seated in front of a poster that featured Jorge's garden, clearly labeled a "communitarian garden." The poster was titled "Problems Identified by the Population" and had been designed to highlight the achievements of the Taller in helping the community meet its needs for recreational space through "the recuperation of vacant lots."[11] The same poster was exhibited, weeks later, at a museum in Habana Vieja also as a way to advertise the kind of integrated community-focused development endorsed by the Office of the Historian.

There were other ways in which GBEA's discursive practices foregrounded the role of the community in the garden, in effect displacing Jorge as the main protagonist in, and ultimate creator of, the space. In GBEA's first newsletter, distributed during the second Spring Festival in 2002, the group was described as "an enthusiastic group of neighbors who, over the last two years, has been meeting and carrying out various actions to better the environment of the neighborhood." The bulletin mentioned Jorge only in a section at the back titled "Children's Section." The text read: "Who are the protagonists of this section? Seventy-five schoolchildren . . . associated with the environmental interest clubs of the neighborhood schools who learn, guided by their teachers and the charismatic and well-known Jorge, neighbor of [name of his street] and caretaker of the Neighborhood Model Garden on [name of the streets]." The leadership ascribed to Jorge in an earlier version of the bulletin had vanished from the text. Rather than being described as a "community leader" (*líder comunitario*) and the creator of the garden, as suggested at some meetings, he was now just a neighbor and caretaker of the site. Jorge did not seem to be bothered as he skimmed the bulletin at the festival and found himself relegated to footnote status in a section that focused primarily on the activities of the schoolchildren. Although at times he complained about how he ran out of his sugar quota to make courtesy herbal refreshments for the children, and he confessed to being exhausted by the three weekly meetings with the schools, he enjoyed his "community work" at the garden.

It took almost a year for Jorge to get a water tank, irrigation hoses, and small wooden stools for the children through CIERIC's funding. Some items, like the metal ladder he so wished for, never materialized. Despite this situation, Jorge kept his commitment to the project and so did the neighbors who participated in the GBEA, including the school-teachers. Jorge was proud of having taught the children "to love the soil" and was delighted that a few of them came by regularly, even after school hours. That for the children the garden represented the closest link with "nature" in their barrio was clear when most of them spontaneously chose the garden as their subject for an art competition on the topic of "the environment" organized by the Office of the Historian in 2002 (see Figure 5.2). Even though none of the drawings featured him, Jorge understood them as a testament to his work. Work at the garden, however, was increasingly presented as, and in some ways was indeed becoming, the work of the community.

The 2002 bulletin claimed to be the voice of the project: "Your voice, my voice . . . ours!" The protagonist of the bulletin was, of course, the community presented as an anonymous mass grounded in the locality. In previous official rhetoric, as mentioned earlier, the faceless and homogenized multitude conjured up by the phrase *el pueblo* (the people) had been commonly eulogized as the vital force of development. Now, in the scaled-down dreams of Special Period Cuba, el barrio or *la comunidad* (the neighborhood or local community), rooted in specific localities, was taking center stage.

The emphasis on small-scale community development perfectly matched the ideal working scale for international funding organizations

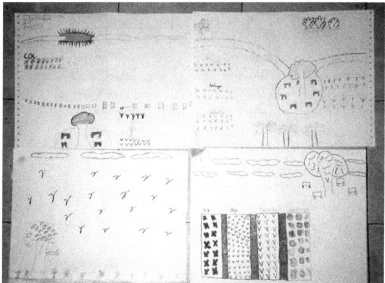

Figure 5.2. Children's drawings for school art competition.

based in capitalist countries, which preferred to support one-time, small, localized initiatives on the island. These not only were "cheap" to fund but also avoided the political conundrum of seemingly cooperating with a government that, to say the least, was and still is controversial in international circles.

Putting aside the appeal for foreign funders, the emphasis on community here also had a particular resonance for Cubans, connecting as it did with long-established models for good socialist conduct that, as mentioned in Chapter 2, privileged the group over the individual. For someone like Jorge, who had already led a full life as an exemplary socialist citizen and who had enthusiastically volunteered in government campaigns, served as president of his neighborhood CDR, and been named a model worker at his former workplace, sacrificing for the greater good appeared to come naturally.

The Practice of Sharing and Its Rewards

Juliana expressed respect and admiration for Jorge as she explained how he was "an incredible neighborhood resource because, even before our appearance on the scene, he already employed a communitarian approach: many people in the community already made use of, and benefited from, his garden." Jorge himself, in his conversations with me, had already underscored this "communitarian approach" to his garden, commenting on how, in the mid-1990s, he had donated a portion of the condiments produced on-site to a neighborhood home for the elderly and had ever since freely shared condiments and medicinal herbs with neighbors who asked for them. Tellingly, when he told me about his desire to have a guava tree, he added, "[I want the tree] not to charge for the fruit but to give it away, because what I like is to give."

In a context where for decades contributing to "the greater good" was upheld as the highest possible value and where, at any rate, the act of giving had always been the basis for sealing alliances, Jorge's public sharing practices were not so surprising. Yet at a time when many felt that hoarding and profiting from food had become the norm, this kind of sharing did appear exceptional, particularly when it encompassed not just friends and relatives but also the community.

There was no doubt that Jorge sincerely enjoyed sharing with others, but it was also evident that he knew his sharing allowed him to amass the "symbolic capital" (Bourdieu 1977) that would help him to keep the site. Explicitly connecting his sharing with the communitarian (read *public*) land tenure status of his lot, he told me,

> I made that garden with the purpose of giving to neighbors what I could, free of charge. . . . My dream is everyone's dream. If you ask my wife, she will tell you the same thing: the dream is to have a beautiful garden, that everyone comments on it [for] it serves to meet everyone's needs because, remember, that this is all communitarian, which means it is for everyone . . . and serving others is the most important thing you can do.

Making an even more explicit connection between his sharing and his insecure land tenure status, speaking of the early donations he made to the retirement home, Jorge mentioned that the manager of this institution had given him several documents acknowledging his generosity, "just in case [he] ever needed them."

As it turned out, he was never asked to show these papers, but his voluntary sharing made all the difference when it came to defending his site. Juliana smiled as she recounted how one of the neighbors who had wanted the garden replaced by a domino playing ground became one of the garden's biggest fans after Jorge gave him some medicinal herbs that helped him treat a respiratory ailment. She openly commented on how important such sharing was to their ability to "save" the garden. She recounted:

> We [at the Taller] argued that it was good to have someone like Jorge in charge of a site like this because he freely and spontaneously was willing to do something healthy and good for everyone; because,

on top of everything, Jorge had such a communitarian and coop-
erative aptitude, such willingness to integrate his effort with those
of others. We argued that he was a real community asset and represented the "intangible values" the Taller wished to uphold in the
community.[12] In this manner, we found a way to legitimate and legalize his situation.

As Juliana's statement illustrated, a communitarian vocation made it
easy to legitimate sites that might otherwise be destroyed to make way
for other city functions. That this was the case beyond the territory of
Habana Vieja was confirmed by the words of an employee of the Provincial Urban Planning Office, who explained to me in March 2001 that
once a parcela became embedded in the territory through its active linkage with community-based activities, it was "more difficult to remove it,
showing a tendency toward permanency."

Emphasizing a garden's communitarian dimension was important to
parceleros in general, who, in contrast with patio owners, often mentioned to me and others how they shared plentiful fruit and medicinal
herbs with neighbors free of charge. It was evident that the continued
rights of parceleros over public land depended, at least in part, on their
ability to make publicly recognized contributions to the community that
proved the value of the production site beyond mere private benefit.
Even in the most "private" of parcelas, the sites' permanency appeared
to ultimately rest not just on the judgment of official authorities who
could be mobilized in their defense but also on the will and needs of the
immediate community.[13]

Sharing in this context was not only "voluntarily" performed by independent actors; it was rewarded by institutional players and reinforced
by the approval of the community. In the end, as will be illustrated in
the next section, it seemed to me that despite the pragmatic and self-
serving motives that might have guided the actions of those involved,
the emphasis on a noncapitalist, communitarian ethos here was, at least
in part, guided by individuals' sincere belief in the superiority of values
that had until recently been central to state discourses and practices.

Reproducing Socialist Values:
Moving beyond the Self

The 2001 Spring Festival, celebrated on May 14, was the first time Jorge's garden was showcased for the public. The garden was not in great shape: the soil was very dry, and there were few plants growing in it. To enliven the display, two of the guinea pigs raised by Jorge were brought down in a cage from his terrace and placed under a sickly avocado tree complete with "an intravenous pouch" that fascinated the children. A few young volunteers from one of the schools that participated in the garden showed up to showcase the educational function of the site. Three attended with a big scrapbook prepared by one of their teachers, which included sample leaves from garden plants and listed their nutritional and medicinal qualities. I asked them to pose for a picture to record the display for posterity.

For a couple of hours, we waited for curious visitors, trying to find cover under the avocado tree that offered little shade. Two tree stumps acted as chairs for those who wanted to take a break. A few of the people who had come out to enjoy the spring festivities came into the garden, but no one stayed for long. The mood was one of lethargy until a crew of television journalists entered the garden.

While Jorge and the children had been expecting the TV crew, they had not been coached on what was expected of them. It became clear that the lead journalist, a blond woman in her thirties named Rosa, was particularly interested in interviewing the schoolchildren. One of them was Jorge's granddaughter, Lisa, a little girl with blond hair and freckles. On being asked why she came to the garden, Lisa responded: "Because my grandpa started this. My grandpa gets the children to come here and teaches them about the garden." The journalist brusquely interrupted Lisa and told her that she was not interested in hearing about Lisa's grandfather but instead wanted to hear about the garden itself and what Lisa and other children did there—for example, she suggested, "how they came to appreciate nature." Lisa, a very bright girl, seemed momentarily humiliated but quickly got the message and performed accordingly for the interview. Like the other two children present, she was sure to mention the importance of the garden in teaching them, as *pioneros* (revolutionary schoolchildren), about love of nature and agriculture and about the nutritious qualities of vegetables—something that, as mentioned earlier, was emphasized in a government campaign of the time. Jorge—his generosity, his relationship to Lisa, and his fundamental role in the garden—was ignored in this official account that instead underscored community participation, civic education, and environmentalism. The social contribution of the parcela itself was highlighted, as if it existed "by the grace of God," as Juliana once commented, rather than through the labor and commitment of an individual who not only invested time in the project but also dedicated some of his meager resources to make the activities a success.

Rosa had featured other gardeners I knew in her TV programs, and so, months later, I interviewed her about her programming choices. She explained that what moved her to focus on parcelas and patios were the "human interest stories" that emerged from those sites. Organopónicos and other commercially oriented urban agriculture sites were too impersonal, "too much like formal workplaces," she explained; parcelas and patios, on the other hand, better illustrated what urban agriculture had already contributed to the community. Beyond supplementing the Cuban family's diet during hard times, these sites, she insisted,

> gave Cuban families the hope that yes, "it could be done" (*se puede*), that yes, one could produce in extreme conditions, that yes, we could survive. But beyond that they helped socialize neighborhoods at a time when people were too centered on their own difficulties to care about others. In such times, these places united the family—not only the family, but the community. And from these interactions and exchanges were born many communitarian projects. I think this is their most fundamentally valuable contribution.

This journalist's emphasis on community contribution was reproduced in many reports by the state media and, as mentioned earlier, was also a predominant component of the discourses of urban agriculture officials and parceleros. Contrary to what a cynical reading might

suggest, there seemed to be more at play here tha
officially endorsed rhetoric. While Rosa clearly triec
gramming relevant to current government campaig.
(hence her emphasis on nature, environmental educa
puede slogan), her insistence on representing the powei
was driven by her own sense of what was valuable about   ...ie
filmed. Her own sense of what deserved to be highlighted   .is probably
a result of many experiences, including her own school years at a time
when *la revolución* was also much younger and hope for building a better society abounded. Whatever the source of her sentiments, what was
clear was that her choices, like those of the elderly gardeners at the El
Cerro clinic, were guided by a desire to find hope and group solidarity
at a time when economic hardship had left people "too centered on their
own difficulties to care about others." Her TV programs showed that yes,
it could be done, that in fact people had found ways to care for each
other in times of acute scarcity. For all the continuity with revolutionary
values that had been institutionally reinforced for decades, however, this
emphasis on sharing and caring for others also had new resonances. Specifically, it hinted at new modes of governance and new forms of citizen
engagement linked to the openings made possible by the Special Period.

Decentering the State:
Different Modes of Engagement

Long before Rafael and Antonio got involved in Jorge's garden, they had
become convinced that permaculture could solve the environmental
and social problems affecting many of Havana's neighborhoods. When
they first met, Rafael was already a well-known, seasoned permaculture
enthusiast who had lectured for the FANJNH and had inspired many to
start their own garden projects. Then, Antonio was a novice in the field
but had the time and interest to dedicate himself to a range of environmental projects. Educated as a hydraulic engineer, he had found himself without a job at the height of the Special Period, yet, through his
affiliation with the Communist Youth, he had secured a spot in a course

that taught him the skills to become a documentary filmmaker with a focus on the environment. Antonio seemed to be sincerely committed to a vision for change in Cuba that resonated with ideas then still being debated, both in and outside political circles, regarding the need for decentralization and for "true" engagement of the population in decision making. He explained, "Unfortunately, there is not a single [government] program that could support the kind of project we are after, which involves implementing the national environmental agenda at the level of local communities."[14] He felt human resources were not an issue in Cuba, where neighborhoods were truly "mixed" and would always have within them people with pertinent skills and expertise. What was needed, he believed, in addition to money, was a different way of operating: "More than create gardens, we are trying to bring about a transformation in people and in the decision-making structures at the local level, very close to the ground. . . . The question is: How can we make it possible for the local community to make decisions? The typical model is to bring directives from above, but I hope that we can share information and motivate people rather than tell them what to do."

Notably, in their idealized depictions of the present and in their hope for the future, Antonio and Rafael, as well as Rosa and Juliana—all in their thirties or forties—did not see the state as an active player in the solution of community problems: in fact, what mattered most to them was that the community learn to help itself with its own human resources and, even when receiving financial assistance from without, that it learn to make decisions for itself. For them, one of the central lessons of the Special Period had been the urgent need to continue decentralizing not just food production but also decision making in general in a manner that would transform the latter into a more participatory and grassroots process. That they all believed in the importance of the environment, as well as in a more engaged community participation, was a sign of the times, which in part reflected pressures exerted by foreign funders and, in part, illustrated important changes in state policies and goals that, as discussed earlier, departed considerably from pre-1989 norms.

Prior to 1989, when the government had more resources at its disposal, it had emphasized large-scale and centralized projects, with little concern for their environmental impact. Notwithstanding exceptional experiments, like the Talleres, which explicitly attempted to encourage participatory urban planning, government-endorsed projects further discouraged the "independent" organization of neighbors into self-contained groups that could generate their own solutions and projects, instead emphasizing nationwide plans that went hand in hand with nationalist sentiments. Now the government was not only prioritizing the previously ignored environmental dimension of healthy urban communities but also encouraging local initiatives that built attachment to the locality, while allowing for greater participation from citizens in decisions that affected their immediate vicinity. Arguably, community projects like the one that involved Jorge's parcela benefited the government in direct ways. First, the community's reclaiming of state land as public land in the manner described here countered what some officials felt were dangerous privatization trends initiated in the early 1990s. Second, by making individuals (as opposed to government institutions) responsible for the welfare of local communities, these kinds of projects allowed the freeing up of state resources for other purposes.

All these benefits notwithstanding, from the official perspective described in Chapter 2, this kind of community participation was far from desirable if allowed to become too independent from state control. The possibility of projects whose objectives ran counter to state interests or made the current state bureaucracy irrelevant seemed to be a concern, even though most sites never strayed too far from the state's formal sphere of influence. In the case of Jorge's parcela, for example, not only were the actions of the community ultimately mediated by an officially recognized institution with clear links to the government (the Office of the Historian of the City), but the local government body (Poder Popular) never completely withdrew its final authority over the site. Thus, following Jorge's death in 2004 and Juliana's departure for Spain on a scholarship in 2005, the site was handed over to a renowned Cuban governmental organization charged with the protection and recuperation of the Bay of Havana. This organization, aided by funding procured from international bodies like the Canadian Embassy, continued Jorge's work with the schools, running a recycling project that involved composting

Figure 5.3. The site of Jorge's parcela 2011.
Photograph courtesy of Nicole Noel.

household waste for the garden. After this recycling project was completed, the representative of the Poder Popular, not the Taller, authorized the site's cultivation by a salaried worker (see Figures 5.3 and 5.4).

Although some would argue that the site continued to function for the benefit of the broader community, in 2009 Jorge's widow, María, bitterly complained that now an individual, rather than the barrio, was benefiting from the lot created and maintained by her late husband. What bothered her most was that the man supervising the garden was rumored to be illegally selling some of its produce at a nearby agricultural market. She protested: "You know we never charged a penny for anything. This isn't right." That María's complaint ended with her mentioning that the Poder Popular now had the key to the garden gate and had given it to this man underscored how the ultimate reclaiming of the site by the government was, in this case, ironically accompanied by the rise of a project that appeared to leave few traces of the garden's recent communitarian function.

Figure 5.4. The entrance to the new garden, 2011.
Photograph courtesy of Nicole Noel.

This final transformation of Jorge's garden serves to highlight the apparently contradictory positions taken by state actors that, on the one hand, endorse community contribution and embeddedness in the field of urban agriculture and, on the other, sometimes seem to stand in its path. This apparent contradiction, in the case of Jorge's parcela, might have been based on the government's growing concern with economic efficiency and productivity, yet, in other cases, as will become evident in the next chapter, these contradictions in the actions of government representatives could in part be explained by the fear of growing independence from the official bureaucracy and its associated controls, a fear that seemed especially pronounced among low-level bureaucrats.

6

Private Plots, Needed Dollars, State Power, and Sustainability Models

Prior to his involvement in Jorge's garden and at the day clinic mentioned in Chapter 3, Rafael had gotten the attention of many in the city for having transformed the cement patio of his home in the municipality of El Cerro into an idyllic edible garden. Placing old truck tires of different sizes one atop the other, he had created terrace-like areas where he cultivated a variety of crops including taro, yams, tomatoes, lettuce, spinach, parsley, basil, oregano, thyme, tarragon, and even turmeric—a spice hardly known in Cuba (Figure 6.1). His love for ornamental plants, particularly orchids, could be seen in his careful placement of these among the food crops. He was proud of his orchids and also of his "sacrificial plants," which he had cultivated as bait for unwanted pests. Rafael credited his garden design to the permaculture classes he had taken with the FANJNH, which had introduced him to the notion of sustainable agriculture. There Rafael had learned about composting, natural pest control, the benefits of intercropping, the practicality of curvilinear design, and the advantages of working with "closed systems" of production that could turn garden "waste" into food.

Unlike Jorge, who was a poor permaculture student, Rafael excelled at implementing (and experimenting with) permaculture design principles. He had the advantage of owning the space he cultivated and so, in theory, had more freedom than Jorge in deciding what to do on the site. He also had the fortune of working in the less crowded municipality of El Cerro, whose greater availability of private and public open spaces

Figure 6.1. Rafael's patio, 2001.

meant that urban agriculture not only was more commonly practiced there but also had long been officially endorsed.[1]

The distinctive location and land tenure status of their gardens notwithstanding, Jorge and Rafael differed significantly from each other in their personal attributes. Rafael was a generation younger than Jorge, and his political views and personal ambitions were quite different. Rafael had never been an active member of his neighborhood CDR and, in general, did not feel particularly attached to the "revolutionary project." Unlike Jorge, who was rather shy and did not consciously network, Rafael actively cultivated both local and global connections that would help him to meet his goals. Over time, these goals included implementing a more sustainable production site, creating a neighborhood garden network, and starting a related Community Information Exchange Center in his home garage, complete with a library, a television, and even a computer and VCR—electronic equipment that is still difficult for Cubans to acquire.

Like Jorge, Rafael did not have the material resources to carry out his "garden dreams." As a caretaker of a garden in a nearby school and later as the coordinator of the garden at the clinic for the elderly, he earned about 170 pesos a month. He occasionally supplemented this income with his share of his family's informal ice sales to neighbors, remittances from relatives abroad, and the sale of some of his food animals, but none of it was sufficient to fund his ambitious garden plans. For this, he depended on institutional assistance.

This chapter illustrates the resilience of patios as it follows Rafael's path toward securing this institutional assistance. Among other things, the chapter illustrates how private producers, like Rafael, can advantageously manage their collaborations with internationally funded NGOs and state institutions in order to achieve personal goals. This analysis shows that while private producers are ultimately subject to some of the same pressures and constraints that guide the actions of parceleros, they are better able to insinuate their own plans into the "dominant" script. Yet, at least some of the time, the compromises patio owners must make to gain official endorsement paradoxically strengthen the very structures of power that might eventually work against their independent plans. Moreover, if acting in ways that circumvent established power hierarchies, patio owners can quickly be reminded that they cannot act as independent actors, especially when collaborating with foreign institutions.

Practicing Permaculture: Cultivating Connections

Ever since 1997, when the FANJNH offered Rafael his first permaculture class, he has considered himself a garden activist, happy to connect with others who share similar interests in growing plants and raising animals. For a while, Rafael collaborated closely with the FANJNH as this institution, in an attempt to encourage his permaculture work, provided him with soil, seeds, tools, advice, and even occasional work opportunities. As he received public recognition for the work he did on his home patio, he became more and more concerned about establishing connections in the broader field of urban agriculture—a field he felt he could excel in. In part because of Rafael's "informality" and in part because of his resentment over unmet expectations of permanent employment, his relationship with the FANJNH had its tensions, yet, through the years, he was able to retain this connection and to cultivate many others with similar officially recognized institutions that could help him achieve his goals. Among these institutions were the local Neighborhood Transformation Workshop, the Juan Tomás Roig Cuban Botanical Association, the Cuban Association for Animal Production (ACPA), and GDIC. In cooperation with these institutions Rafael lectured on permaculture, gave talks about the advantages of raising guinea pigs, participated in the Annual Agricultural Fair of Havana, gave television interviews, and welcomed to his garden numerous Cuban and foreign visitors.

By the early 2000s, Rafael had achieved such fame in Havana's urban agriculture field that high-ranking individuals in GDIC, ACPA, Havana's Urban Agriculture Department, and the Provincial Headquarters of Urban Planning all mentioned his name during interviews without my prompting. His work had even received the attention of the then newly created Ministerio de Ciencia, Tecnología y Medioambiente (Ministry of Science, Technology, and the Environment, CITMA), in charge of Cuba's environmental policy, which had awarded Rafael a monetary prize to assist with his garden project. Since this ministry could not release the funds directly to a private individual and Rafael could not find an official institution with an authorized bank account to oversee his garden project, he was never able to access this money. Nevertheless, he remained hopeful that he would eventually find the financial support required to carry out his ambitious garden plan.

Although Rafael preferred working with NGOs, he felt networking with official state institutions could never hurt since these connections would only lend further legitimacy to his work. Thus it was not surprising that as soon as he heard about the launching of the official Patio and Parcela Movement, he expressed a desire to participate by joining the national competition for the title of model garden known as *patio* or *parcela de referencia*. This title carried little or no material incentive, but, as just suggested, it could become a source of needed "symbolic capital."

The Movement to Green Urban Agriculture

Like many other small-scale urban farmers in Havana, Rafael heard about the Patio and Parcela Movement through a MINAG representative who visited his place and left behind a pamphlet that advertised the related garden competition. This pamphlet outlined the vision for these kinds of sites endorsed by its official sponsors, the MINAG and the CDRs. It stated that an ideal model patio or parcela was one that functioned as a positive example to other families in the surrounding neighborhood for the quality of the "subprograms," or production components, it contained. These components embodied the ideal garden as a site characterized by a diverse mixture of crops and animals, the use of nonchemical solutions for problems such as soil infertility, the optimal recycling of household and production-related "waste" through practices such as composting, and the conscious promotion of other environmentally sound practices. Each of the various categories of crops—medicinal plants, salad greens, fruit trees, or root crops, for example—constituted a different subprogram. The list of subprograms also included activities like beekeeping; aquaculture; raising fowl, rabbits, and guinea pigs; soil conservation; and the production of organic matter and animal feed. There was even a subprogram labeled *medioambiente* (environment), created to acknowledge activities conducted on a patio or parcela that contributed to the environmental health of the surrounding community (Companioni et al. 2002).

In its broad outlines, this ideal garden in part coincided with that promoted by NGOs like the FANJNH, which, as mentioned earlier, had already influenced Rafael's work. On closer consideration, however, there were notable differences. While FANJNH workshops did not appear to succeed at converting producers to the overall philosophy associated with permaculture, they did appear to have convinced their participants that they needed to understand how the different components of the garden might fit together to create a balanced production system. By contrast, even though those working in the urban agriculture sector at higher levels of the MINAG no doubt understood how the subprograms needed to fit together to create a sustainable production site, the manner in which the model gardens competition was conducted turned the whole idea of biodiversity, for example, into a mere exercise of adding isolated elements into the garden without much thought about their possible interactions.[3]

MINAG municipal delegates and district representatives, who preselected model gardens, consistently emphasized quantity of subprograms as being key to the selection process, even though the movement's brochures and its leadership at the national and provincial levels emphasized quality over quantity of subprograms.[2] Describing the three gardens preselected at the level of his municipality, the delegate from Centro Habana, for example, explained that they were chosen "because they contained from eight to ten subprograms." The municipal delegate for El Cerro also stated that to be considered for selection, a patio "must have *at least* four to five subprograms out of the twenty-two present in the municipality" (emphasis mine). A representative working in her municipality was even more demanding, categorically stating that "those selected have to have from nineteen to twenty-two of the existing twenty-four subprograms." The delegate for Centro Habana did not specify the number of subprograms required for selection, but Raquel, one of the representatives working in his territory, while not stipulating a minimum required quota of subprograms, did emphasize that a diversity of subprograms was important: "To be considered a model garden, one must first have a variety of subprograms, of which as you know there are a possible total of twenty-seven." While, clearly, perception on this issue varied from municipality to municipality and from individual to individual, there seemed to be a general consensus that quantity of subprograms did matter, at least for those in the middle and lower strata of the decision-making hierarchy.

The weight that this MINAG ideal of sustainable agriculture had even on producers who worked in private spaces became clear to me as Rafael prepared for a series of visits related to the official movement.

Falling in Line with Official Standards

Transformative Acts of Integration

In March 2001, Rafael found out that none other than Contino, the national president of the CDRs, was expected to view his garden as part of a national CDR-MINAG delegation engaged in the process of selecting model patios and parcelas. Weeks earlier, anticipating this visit, he had calmly started planting fruit trees and coffee plants, but on the day of the visit he was overcome with anxiety. He complained that there remained too much to be done and persuaded his sister and three friends, including me, to help with the preparations. Within a few hours, the garden was "cleaned up"[4] and a pond was created where Rafael could keep fish acquired from a neighbor.

In the end, Contino did not show up and Rafael's garden was not selected as a model patio after this official visit, still the garden was considered sufficiently outstanding to be included in a tour of El Cerro given to a delegation of model gardeners from Matanzas province who came to Havana in September 2001 to attend the First Annual National Meeting of the Patio and Parcela Movement. About six months had elapsed since Rafael's garden had been evaluated for the competition, and very little had changed at the site until a few days prior to the visit. Then, the garden once again underwent considerable transformations. Rafael prominently exhibited a couple of caged guinea pigs that were actually only temporarily in his care (his own, less healthy-looking guinea pigs were hidden away in an inner courtyard). Among his garden crops he had interspersed a series of didactic signs carrying messages that echoed those of the movement and emphasized the environmental dimension of the garden. One of them read, "Organic agriculture: a sustainable way of life." Another stated, "A healthy environment guarantees your health" (see Figure 6.2). The changes did not just involve production-related elements but also added a political dimension to Rafael's garden. In a bright and clean sitting area, recently created following the destruction of a dilapidated and long-unused chicken coop, Rafael had even hung a picture of Che Guevara.

Figure 6.2. Ministry of Agriculture–related slogans in Rafael's patio, 2001.

In Rafael's case, the timing of these changes to coincide with visits from movement officials, as well as the types of transformations, made it evident that he was trying to live up to what he understood to be the MINAG and CDR ideals. Like many other producers, Rafael understood that the criterion of "biodiversity" was measured by the MINAG through a mere count of the subprograms present in a given garden. Consequently, his inclusion of fish, as well as his recent addition of coffee plants, fruit trees, and guinea pigs, increased by three the already considerable number of subprograms represented in his patio. His self-conscious attempt to re-create the ideal garden as conceived by ministry and CDR officials was only underscored by his strategic use of signs and revolutionary imagery.

From my observations, these kinds of conscious and, at times, cynical attempts to live up to official expectations were not uncommon. According to Manuel, the former representative of agriculture in Santa Fé, this kind of behavior appeared to be encouraged by the MINAG's way of promoting the subprogram system. Describing producers who, to impress MINAG officials, acquired (or simply borrowed) rabbits or ducks for the sole purpose of fulfilling the perceived subprogram requirement, Manuel lamented: "What madness! In this way, everything becomes a great show."

Although there was an element of disingenuous performance in some of the changes producers made before an inspection, it seemed to me, observing Rafael and others, that such transformations at times had a deeper and more lasting impact. While some of the lettuce Rafael replanted near the plantains in new recycled containers quickly dried up, the containers remained and were planted with more suitable crops. The pond became for a while a fixture in Rafael's garden, and he was particularly proud of it. He was convinced that, as permaculture teachings suggested, it had improved the microclimate of the garden. It was clear, then, that while Rafael and others changed their sites just to meet MINAG requirements, they retained some of these changes because they liked them. As the competition continued and some producers aspired to the title of model garden year after year, their approximations of the ideal were only further refined over time.[5] This meant not only the improvement of existing production components but also a conscious effort to link garden work with the environmental health of the larger community as promoted by movement officials.

Socializing Private Gardens

After not receiving the title of model garden in 2001, Rafael was not formally invited to the First Annual National Meeting of the Patio and Parcela Movement, yet he decided to attend the event anyway. Rafael seemed completely at ease during the meeting and listened attentively to the messages delivered by those standing at the podium. Contino, the charismatic national president of the CDRs, passionately pronounced: "We must break with the concept that the patio of my home is private. True, it is private in terms of property rights, but with respect to the benefits it brings to the community it is also social. It benefits all of us, not just through the increased availability of produce; having a good fruit tree in one's patio positively contributes to the overall environment, to the air we breathe." This statement clearly made an impression on Rafael, who was still trying to find support for his neighborhood garden network and related Community Information Center at his home. When other model producers at the meeting began taking turns to comment on their contributions to the movement, Rafael got up and, taking his turn alongside them, began, "Alluding to Contino's words, I want to tell everyone that four years ago the patio at my home stopped being private and became a communitarian patio." He went on to describe how his patio had become a meeting place for producers and a space where many educational workshops on sustainable agriculture had taken place. These, he further explained, had involved adults as well as children: the garden benefited everyone in the community. Before he sat down, he was sure to mention his desire to build a Community Information Center, and, to my surprise, he said its planned location was to be the state hospital where he was then working with the group of elderly outpatients. As Rafael passionately spoke about his dreams, his words indeed evoked the concept of the *Hombre Nuevo* (New Man)—the ideal socialist citizen committed to serving the broader community, as described by the same Che Guevara whose image had materialized in Rafael's garden.

It should be noted that, political ideology aside, helping create a more solidaristic community was an objective that was close to Rafael's heart, as was his conviction that gardening was key to fomenting socially, physically, and emotionally healthy communities. From his first permaculture design in 1997, which featured a commune-like apartment building where each resident would produce an agricultural product to be exchanged with other residents in the building, to his current plans for a communitarian patio, Rafael's dreams reflected a consistent interest in contributing to a caring community. Rafael indeed placed a high value on community-centered activities in general. His nostalgic accounts of life in his hometown often emphasized how everyone shared everything—from food to the raising of children—and even though his resources were meager, he always shared whatever food he had with those who came to visit. This, he felt, was the way things should be. He felt very uncomfortable about charging for food or shelter and often criticized the commodification of human relations that had come about with the onset of the Special Period, complaining about how people had become obsessed with making money, often prioritizing monetary gain over friendships and family. Other members of the neighborhood garden network, including the gardeners on Dawn Street discussed in Chapters 3 and 4, also shared Rafael's desire to build a stronger and more support-ive neighborhood community. In this respect, except for the very differ-ent location noted for the planned Information Center, Rafael's account of his garden work at the meeting of the movement matched what I knew of his plans, and what I myself had witnessed as I participated in the many community activities he regularly organized in his patio.

Despite the parallels Rafael attempted to draw at the meeting between official agendas within the Patio and Parcela Movement and his own garden work, there were notable differences between them. As Antonio had explained, his and Rafael's intention was not "to force" or prescribe anything to those who chose to participate in their garden net-work but rather to allow the network to define and promote the pro-cess of "greening" the city, acting as a forum for knowledge transfer among equals rather than as a transmission belt for directives handed down "from above." Despite the already-mentioned acknowledgment by MINAG officials that their work with producers was above all a job of persuasion rather than prescription, when it came to small-scale urban agriculture sites, community participation and service for those in the movement appeared to be expected to materialize in a dogmatic manner. Thus, the representative of agriculture for Centro Habana, for example, insisted that "[community work] is a collateral fact that derives from the natural development of the movement. Remember that this movement is carried out through the neighborhood CDRs. Hence, the community *has* to participate in the gardens and the gardens *have* to service the com-munity" (emphasis original).

Rafael's very different conception of community participation notwithstanding, he was not at the meeting to point out the contrasts between his vision and that of state bureaucrats. Rather, he was there to publicly show how his project fit in, and fell in line with, government programs. For this, he was willing to engage in a fair amount of posturing and exaggeration—behavior that was almost expected at this kind of public political gathering. Indeed, it seemed that every producer in attendance was vying for attention from officials with ever more exuberant accounts of their gardening accomplishments.

Agricultural Tall Tales: Standing Out from the Rest
There were many instances, particularly at public meetings, when it was difficult not to agree with Manuel's statement that, in the insane drive to meet official expectations, in Cuba "everything becomes a great show." The meeting of the Patio and Parcela Movement provided me with ample evidence of this.

I knew from talking to producers who were suddenly showing interest in fruit trees that beginning in 2000 the MINAG had begun placing particular emphasis on the fruit tree subprogram. The subprogram had as its aim the recuperation of local varieties of fruit trees through encouraging their cultivation in the city. To facilitate this goal, the ministry promoted the creation of nurseries and made efforts to ensure that tree seedlings were part of the "protected products" offered by all TCAs throughout the city. At the time, tree seedlings were also made available at nurseries or at city fairs organized regularly by entities such as the National Botanical Garden of Cuba, and many of the producers I knew appeared to welcome such opportunities.

Like other subprograms promoted by the ministry, the fruit tree subprogram for the Patio and Parcela Movement had optimistic projected production quotas (*metas*) attached to it. These were mentioned repeatedly at the meeting where Contino excitedly proclaimed, "The contributions patios can make here are immense; extraordinary, really. With this idea, in a relatively short time we could *fill Cuba with fruit*, comrades" (emphasis his).

One of the producers present at the meeting appropriately warned: "We have to be careful here. It is not a matter of having one hundred fruit trees in a four-by-four-meter patio. It is about having those that fit in order to be productive." But his statement was lost in the enthusiastic reporting of many others who boasted about the number of fruit trees they had managed to squeeze into a limited space.

As I sat recording the proceedings, Rafael was seated to my right. To my left was Rodrigo, a longtime acquaintance of Rafael's. As the meeting went on, they conversed across me. As a producer from Santiago was telling the audience about the incredible number of trees he had on his small patio, Rafael turned to Rodrigo and mockingly said, "I bet you the trees do not bear a thing." At another point, as we listened to Adolfito, the president of the National Urban Agriculture Department, provide statistics on the magnitude of production coming out of patios, Rafael turned again to Rodrigo and boastfully stated, "Did I tell you I already have eighteen fruit trees on my patio?" Minutes later, as he stood up to tell the story of his garden, three more fruit trees had been added to the count! He announced: "Only 10 percent of my patio has soil. Yet I have twenty-one different fruit trees planted there!"

While Rafael often criticized in private the exaggerated production statistics presented by the MINAG, in this situation he seemed to be more than willing to participate. The same seemed to be true of other producers I knew in the audience. If, as I suspected, everyone present was aware of the exaggerated nature of some production claims, what purpose did these tall tales serve?

On the one hand, individually the statements might be considered an attempt to get the attention and approval of those officials present at the meeting by underscoring the individual producer's competence. On the other hand, together they had the effect of a chorus that reaffirmed the allegiance of those present, not just to specific production goals espoused by the ministry but to the continued struggle against all odds captured in Raúl Castro's slogan that *se puede* (it can be done). Thus, a producer from Havana province, for example, commenting on the fruit tree subprogram, stated:

This is a program that is just beginning, but three years from now we are talking about tons and tons of fruit. . . . This will be a gradual development, but as far as I am concerned I will not stop and will not be happy until I hear it said on television that we no longer have to import guava fruit [and] that the Cuban factories are working again and producing without having to spend a dollar overseas. In a forty-meter patio one can nurse twenty thousand guava plants. . . . And we are not only speaking of guavas, but of peaches, cinnamon—all things that are imported and that we can grow here. I am willing to share all I know toward this goal. In the future, there will be hundreds of such nurseries that will produce two million guavas. Then you will see that, as one of our comrades from Havana province says, airplanes will have difficulty landing in Cuba, their visibility being clouded by the flies attracted to the sweetness of our land! Yes, it can be done (*se puede*)!

This producer's emphasis on his personal commitment to ensure the well-being of the nation by contributing to Cuba's self-sufficiency in fruit had clear political overtones, as did Rafael's own direct reference to the words of the national CDR president, his wearing of a T-shirt with a CDR logo at the meeting, and his earlier display of Che's image on his patio. On the one hand, Rafael's conscious re-creation of his patio not just as a MINAG-approved model of sustainability but also as a politically integrated space underscored the compromises he was willing to make to obtain official recognition to serve his own ends of amassing support for his garden projects. On the other hand, these personal political strategies arguably had the effect of reinforcing the power of the state by publicly legitimating its projects. That, in Rafael's case, these acts of allegiance were not completely sincere did not seem to matter since the overall effect of such a public show of acquiescence, particularly when known to involve even those citizens least aligned with the government, only reasserted the authority of the MINAG in this field and, through it, the power of the state. How the enactment of state power here went hand in hand with producers' desires to legitimate their own production sites was particularly illustrated in the voluntary public display of movement-related signs and diplomas on garden gates, home doors, and house walls.

Signs of Acquiescence: Legitimating Moves

After the representatives of agriculture began their census of small-scale urban agriculture sites, in part designed to bring into view those gardens that could then be considered for the title of *patio* or *parcela de referencia*, the movement acquired visibility across the city as related signs began to appear on home doors and garden gates. The signs, some of which were even printed in color, read: "This house participates in the Popular Movement for Agricultural Production of the Neighborhood, by the Neighborhood, and for the Neighborhood. United we will win this battle as part of the war of the people" (see Figure 1.2). As I accompanied the representative of agriculture for El Cerro on his daily rounds, I learned that these signs were not placed there by functionaries carrying out the census. Rather, they were voluntarily displayed by the producers themselves who were asked (not required) to put the signs up. This voluntary act, when it happened, was telling since the signs did more than mark inclusion in the census: they publicly underscored the integration of the producer and related site into the official program endorsed by the government, explicitly linking both to the discursive construction of urban agriculture as part of the revolutionary struggle—an act with clear political implications.

There were other important physical signs that underscored the integration of producers into official programs in general. These included the diplomas of merit received by those who won the title of model garden, as well as the institutional certificates and logos that further signaled producers' collaborations with officially approved NGOs working in the field. These signs were proudly displayed on house walls, not just in recognition of the help received but also as a way to demonstrate to others the site's legitimacy and the producer's credibility. This, as will be seen, was particularly important for producers like Rafael who wanted to use their gardens as a starting point for broader community projects. After all, the producers felt that being perceived as respectful of officially recognized players in the field was the key to success.

Minding Established Power Hierarchies

As we exited the First Annual National Meeting of the Movement, Rafael and I accepted a ride home from Vilda Figueroa and José (Pepe) Lama, a couple whose work in the municipality of Marianao had inspired Rafael to fantasize about opening a Community Information Exchange Center for gardeners. Years earlier, in 1996, Vilda and Pepe had started a food conservation workshop and accompanying vegetable garden to teach families from their community the skills to cope with acute food insecurity. Their project, known as the Proyecto Comunitario Conservación de Alimentos (PCCA), had soon gained the attention of national and international institutions. Vilda and Pepe told me that they had never explicitly sought international funding for the PCCA, but a number of foreign organizations, including the previously mentioned Agro Acción Alemana (AAA) and the Australian Conservation Foundation (ACF), had approached them to offer assistance. Although this assistance was at times unduly delayed by an overzealous Cuban bureaucracy reluctant to channel foreign aid to locally run projects, it eventually reached the PCCA, allowing Vilda and Pepe to cover the cost of project publications as well as needed office equipment, from computers and printers to VCRs.[6]

Vilda and Pepe were eager to point out the project's viability, independent of such external help. They insisted that the success of the PCCA was first and foremost due to the logistic and material support they received from state institutions and other official organisms whose logos often appeared on their published materials. The CDRs had been instrumental in helping them disseminate information on gardening and food preservation. Likewise, the MINAG had helped by printing brochures and assisting with their distribution nationwide. The official Radio Ciudad de La Habana had even given them air time for their own weekly radio show. To Vilda and Pepe, working with state institutions and in alignment with existing political structures made absolute sense. For Rafael, however, things were a bit more complicated.

As we rode back with the couple after the meeting, Rafael first congratulated them on their brand-new car, but, a while later, behind their back, he humorously referred to them as the Aeroflot couple. When I asked Rafael to tell me why he had used the name of the Russian airline to describe them, he explained, laughing, "Because they travel places!" This joke alluded to Vilda and Pepe's worldly connections (from the ACF to the AAA), which, in the view of Rafael and others, enabled their social and physical mobility. The nickname simultaneously hinted at this couple's previous travel experience in the Soviet Union (they had studied there) while underscoring their public allegiance to socialism and the communist party (hence the reference to Aeroflot rather than, say, Iberia). At a time in Cuba when owning a new car, having a computer-equipped office, traveling overseas, and corresponding with foreigners were rare privileges, Vilda and Pepe had achieved a great deal. Rafael's comment only underscored how their achievements were seen to result not just from their enthusiasm, resourcefulness, and creativity but also from their positioning in relation to preexisting national power networks. There was no doubt that, at this historical juncture, connections, particularly with the "capitalist world," were becoming more common in Cuba than they had been since the first years of revolutionary rule. Still, such connections, while unsettling established power hierarchies within the country, could not (and did not) eliminate them. As Rafael knew all too well, official government institutions and "state gatekeepers" (Corrales 2004) still retained the power to legitimate transnational exchanges and, ultimately, legalize the possession and use of things like new computers and cars in Cuba. Despite all the signs of change, these state actors could still enable—or crush—even the most painstakingly constructed of garden dreams. Here, the personal trajectory of producers and their perceived integration into the revolutionary process appeared to matter a great deal.

The Making and Unmaking of Garden Dreams

In 2004, Rafael earned the title of model garden at both the municipal and national levels. By then, his production endeavors had been expanded from his home patio to his rooftop, where he was raising rabbits and guinea pigs and cultivating a variety of crops, including pep-

Figure 6.3. Pepper plants in Rafael's rooftop garden, 2004.

pers, guavas, tomatoes, beans, and grapes (Figures 6.3 and 6.4). With Antonio's assistance, he continued running all sorts of neighborhood-related activities, including monthly gastronomic fairs to teach good eating habits and biweekly meetings with children from three local primary schools. Rafael had secured enough financial support from a range of officially endorsed institutions within Cuba to be able to create a Community Information Exchange Center in his garage. Through ACPA he had received funding from the Rosa Luxemburg Foundation to fix up the garage, and through GDIC he had tapped into international funding to secure a computer—something rarely found in the average Cuban home at the time. The center also had a television and VCR, desks, and a library where Rafael displayed books and brochures on permaculture, nutrition, and the environment. With additional funding and some support from the FANJNH, Rafael had also redone the rooftop area of his home, furnishing it with a kitchen preparation area where he hoped to one day be able to offer cooking and food preservation workshops to the

Figure 6.4. View of Rafael's patio garden below, 2004.

community. As before, he continued to collaborate with local institutions like the Neighborhood Transformation Workshop (TTB), but he was reluctant to work too closely with the CDRs, even turning down the job of representative of agriculture for his district, which would in fact have meant working for the CDR.

Rafael's garden, like many other "model" gardens in the field, had become an established stop for foreigners interested in learning about Havana's urban agriculture experience. These foreign connections had occasionally brought in needed money for small garden-related projects. For example, Rafael and Antonio had received money directly from a European organization to produce a short documentary on Cuban permaculture, which, of course, featured Rafael's own garden. They had also managed to get the neighborhood garden network listed in a global dictionary of sustainability produced by a Dutch environmental NGO. They even had an Internet presence through a friend who managed a website that showcased Cuban community projects for an international audience. Inclusion in this website, as well as in the sustainability dictionary, had no money attached to it but was a source of pride for Rafael and his whole family. I recall his sister's excitement when they received a copy of the sustainability handbook. She showed it to everyone who came to the house that day, saying: "Look! Rafael's garden has now made it into an international book! Who would have thought of it? Little Rafael and his plants!"

Rafael's public recognition and connections, as well as his adamant "freelance" status, had earned him a few enemies. According to Antonio and others I spoke to, the delegate of agriculture from the municipality of El Cerro, in particular, appeared jealous of the resources Rafael had been able to amass on his own. Some members of the FANJNH, in their conversations with me, betrayed disappointment at Rafael's new alliances with other NGOs in the field. Even some participants in Rafael's garden network seemed disappointed at Rafael as they noted how the garden project had resulted in considerable improvements to Rafael's own private home. One day, he was shocked to hear that he was under suspicion of running a counterrevolutionary center at the Community Information Exchange Center in his home. The accusations even made mention of foreigners from the United States and Europe visiting the site and allegedly funding "dubious activities" there. Because just the previous year the government had jailed what it described as seventy-five dissidents, some of whom were said to be running "independent" libraries out of their homes with U.S. government funding, these accusations had scary implications for Rafael and Antonio. In the end, the accusations were unsubstantiated, but they resulted in Rafael losing the computer and other equipment he had secured for the information center. This equipment, he told me, was transferred to the Neighborhood Transformation Workshop in his municipality, which was seen to be better able to oversee its proper public use.

The actual source and motives for the accusation of counterrevolutionary work, and the related confiscation of equipment from Rafael's information center, were difficult for me to ascertain, but what seemed evident from the information I gathered is that Rafael's independent work had annoyed a number of state (and nonstate) actors, many of whom felt he was "duplicating" their work and disrupting the status quo. In its details, what happened to Rafael was certainly unique among the producers I knew, and yet it seemed to fit a pattern that applied to other community garden projects perceived to be encouraging different modes of citizen participation, independent of state institutions. Juliana herself had alluded to the local government's initial suspicions of the work carried out by the Taller in Jorge's parcela in Habana Vieja, telling me that, for this reason, she had made sure to invite organizations, like the CDR, to GBEA's meetings. Going further back in time, there was, of course, Manuel's account of the horticulturalist clubs in Santa Fé, which in the early 1990s, when their popularity was at their peak, were also regarded with suspicion by state actors. According to Manuel, established state-endorsed neighborhood organizations, like the CDRs, not only were threatened by neighborhood meetings that did not report back to them but also simply did not understand the clubs' encouragement of "direct" community participation in decision making. In this context, it is difficult not to think that Rafael was in part punished for his different vision of community participation, one that circumvented official organisms like the CDRs, which Vilda and Pepe said were a building block of their successful program.

Rafael's case further suggested a renewed cycle of political vigilance and control in the mid-2000s that has opened and closed many times since. Such cycles of state vigilance are, of course, not unique to Cuba and are typical of other states especially at times of perceived or imagined crisis (one need look only at government practices in the United States since 9/11 to find plenty of examples of intolerance, generalized paranoia, and a context where unfair accusations can be freely made against all sorts of vulnerable subjects). This is not to say, however, that this incident did not have its own distinctive Cuban flavor. For Rafael, this was definitely not a universal story but his own personal story in his own country—an experience that took a toll on him but never quite dissuaded him from continuing his garden work.

Right after the accusations were made, a great chill descended on Rafael's garden site and home, and he fell into a deep depression, temporarily abandoning his patio. In a few months, however, he was back to his normal self. Over time, those neighbors who at first avoided him returned to visit his home. The Cuban NGOs that had always supported his work, in one way or another, continued to do so because, in the end, they needed Rafael as much as he needed them. Even known government bodies, such as the Grupo de Trabajo Estatal para el Saneamiento, Conservación y Desarrollo de la Bahía de La Habana (State Working Group for the Improvement, Conservation, and Development of the Havana Bay), the same entity that briefly administered a recycling program out of Jorge's garden, lent support to Rafael, who, by 2007, had replaced Che's portrait with a wall-size mural that advertised this organization's environmental work in the city.

I last had a long visit with Rafael in 2009. Then, he continued to talk about the garden and about helping facilitate a network of producers, albeit without the need for an information center. People interested in his garden work, including foreigners, still frequented his patio and received his warm welcome. Such personal connections, after all, not only led to real friendships for Rafael but also, over time, made it possible for him to secure a place for himself within the urban agriculture movement in Cuba and beyond. That his garden was still thriving, and still receiving such attention, points to his resilience as well as to the important role that he, and other model urban farmers like him, have come to play in official representations of urban agriculture tailored to a global audience that, in one way or another, can influence and has influenced what happens in the field in Cuba.

7

Global Networks and
Cuban Urban Agriculture

In November 2008, the FANJNH organized the Third Latin American Permaculture Convention at a camping resort a distance from Havana. In attendance were over forty permaculture enthusiasts from countries like Argentina, Brazil, Colombia, Ecuador, Mexico, Uruguay, Spain, and the United States. Also present at the convention were ninety-four Cubans, including fifty small-scale urban farmers from various parts of the country and employees from the FANJNH, government institutions like the MINAG, and Cuban NGOs like ACPA, CIERIC, and the Cuban Council of Churches.

The producers from Havana represented different barrios, as well as diverse trajectories within the city's urban agriculture movement. There were individuals like Manuel and the dynamic duo, Vilda and Pepe, who, from their respective municipalities of Playa and Marianao, had led community-centered projects (i.e., horticulturalist clubs, agricultural consultancy offices, and food conservation workshops) that greatly impacted the early development of the field. While less influential, also in attendance were a number of parceleros that had been around since the early years of the Special Period. Among them were Pancho, a man of peasant background with a large parcela and a fish breeding pond near the capitol building in Centro Habana and Vivencio, a retired army man with a commercial medicinal plant garden in the central municipality of Plaza. There were also, importantly for the FANJNH, many producers who self-identified as permaculturists. Some were relative novices in the field like Miriam, an agronomist who had recently started coordinating a group of women in Diez de Octubre who wanted to commercialize ornamental plants grown in their permaculture-inspired patios, and Claudio, a retired member of the Cuban mercantile fleet, who had just started experimenting with rabbits, beekeeping, and tilapia on his patio in Habana del Este with the aim of supplementing his family's diet. Finally, there were a number of producers who had been widely recognized for their novel applications of permaculture design like Rafael, with his still-thriving, noncommercial patio in El Cerro, and Manolo, whose rooftop animal production in the same municipality had earned him not just fame but money.

While I was interested in what all of them had to say to an international audience, I was most curious to hear Manolo's presentation, since I knew him to be a good storyteller and thought he had one of the most interesting permaculture experiments in Havana. With the assistance of the FANJNH and ACPA, Manolo had repurposed the rooftop of his home to raise rabbits, guinea pigs, and chickens and cultivate vegetables and herbs.[1] He not only dehydrated the food leftovers from his and another seven neighboring households to make rabbit feed but also further mixed this feed with protein-rich rabbit droppings to serve to his chickens. The grass and other greens his rabbits discarded, on the other hand, fell from their elevated cages to the ground, where it was eaten by the guinea pigs, left to roam freely for this purpose. He was also using a portion of the animal excrement he collected to experiment with vermiculture (raising worms) and regularly fertilized his crops with chicken manure. He even fed worms from his vermiculture experiment to the chickens. His unique implementation of permaculture was a source of pride for the FANJNH, which considered his site one of the obligatory stops on its garden tours.

I expected Manolo's talk to be engaging, but, to my surprise, it was not. He started by dispassionately outlining his production endeavors, giving more information than the audience required about the specific nutritional needs of rabbits. Then he stopped abruptly and asked the audience if they had any questions. In answering one of the questions, he stated, "All that matters to me, in the end, is that waste goes up to my rooftop and comes down as money." Although this statement was truthful, Luis, a member of the FANJNH who worked closely with Manolo, turned to me and whispered, "Geez, he just threw away all the ethical principles of permaculture with a single sentence!"

A young man with a background in agricultural sciences who had previously worked with the Cuban Association for Organic Agriculture (ACAO), Luis did not feel that there was anything wrong with producers making a living through the sale of their produce.[2] However, in this context, Manolo's comments embarrassed him. This was, after all, an international gathering of individuals who, for the most part, felt that caring for nature and for fellow human beings, rather than profit seeking, were the guiding ethical principles of all permaculture practitioners. Manolo's emphasis on profit was out of place here and put into question the effectiveness of FANJNH teachings; hence, Luis's disappointment at Manolo's pronouncements.

This incident, and the meeting in general, made me aware of how important global connections and international repute were, not just for the FANJNH, but for the Cuban urban agriculture movement overall. Without the kinds of global connections established by Cuban NGOs, like the FANJNH, Manolo would never have become a permaculturist. Moreover, it would have been difficult, if not impossible, for him to acquire the material resources that allowed him to develop his site as he did, allowing money to "come down" from the rooftop of his home. The same could be said for many of the others present at the meeting who had, in one way or another, come to benefit from the global connections the FANJNH had established over a decade earlier.

Permaculture as Knowledge That Travels

In 1993, a group of young permaculture activists from Australia and New Zealand traveled to Cuba on a solidarity mission. A couple of them persuaded the director of a government ministry in the well-to-do district of El Vedado, in the municipality of Plaza, to start a rooftop permaculture garden with a small group of interested employees. Among these employees was a middle-aged woman with no agricultural background, named Luisa, and a young biologist in his twenties, named Pablo. Although the garden experience was short-lived (the ministry in question closed its doors as a result of the economic crisis and the permaculture classes were eventually moved to another site elsewhere in the city), it left those who participated, including Luisa and Pablo, convinced that the knowledge of permaculture deserved to be disseminated throughout Havana. The young foreign brigade members returned home to their countries and founded the Cuba Green Team with the objective of seeking funding to promote permaculture on the island. In a move that allowed them to tap into funds from the Australian government's international development agency, AusAid, the Cuba Green Team, joined the ACF. In 1994, as part of the ACF, the Green Team began working with the FANJNH on developing the Cuban Permaculture Project, alongside Luisa and Pablo, both of whom were recruited into the FANJNH with this collaboration in mind. The project was to be coordinated by Graciela, the engineer mentioned in Chapter 1, who through her prior employment in the urban planning sector, had amassed a great deal of experience pertaining to the development of urban agriculture in Havana. The ACF's collaboration with the FANJNH lasted several years and resulted in a series of publications and in the teaching of numerous permaculture workshops and courses—which, initially at least, required the participation of a qualified permaculture instructor from Australia.

This prerequisite of a qualified permaculture instructor meant that, from its inception, the permaculture program at the FANJNH was premised on firsthand participation by Australians. The underlying assumption, at least at the beginning, was that the Australians were reservoirs of a unique body knowledge that was badly needed in Special Period Cuba. This much was reflected in the words of Australian Bill Mollison, one of the fathers of permaculture, who in an interview conducted by Scott Vlaum (2001) suggested that the Cubans had much to learn from Australian permaculturists. He commented how, in the 1990s, he had advised his students headed for Cuba "not to take any notice of . . . what's his name . . . Fidel because he's a notorious brown thumb." Emphasizing his poor opinion of Cuba's prior agricultural policies, Mollison added, "Fidel decided to plant only sugar cane, you know, and left [Cubans] in such a mess." The ability of Cubans to come up with their own indigenous solutions for the "mess" left behind by prior agricultural policies was not directly acknowledged in Mollison's statement, yet it was definitely recognized by those permaculture instructors who spent time in Cuba and who, according to some of the producers I met, often let them know how they (i.e., Cubans) had already intuitively discovered many key practices central to permaculture. According to David Holmgren, the other Australian cofounder of permaculture who, unlike Mollison, spent time in Cuba, permaculture activists working outside Australia did not just deliver knowledge; they also learned from these experiences. In Holmgren's assessment, working in countries like Cuba that had to cope with the kind of serious petroleum shortages that one day might affect nations like Australia held great potential for those interested in the long-term applicability of permaculture systems. He stated, "Permaculture has spread around the world and is already dealing with energy-descent-type situations in other countries. One of the places, for example, where people interested in permaculture go to study that, as much as to help, is Cuba. There you have a society that was quite industrialized, that went into an artificial energy descent because of the collapse of the Soviet Union, and they've actually adapted to that in quite a creative way" (cited in Fenderson 2004). Explicit in this statement, as in the mentioned praise that permaculture instructors gave many Cuban producers, was the recognition that Cubans could in fact contribute to the further development of permaculture.

As all forms of knowledge that travel well, permaculture, much like the river stream described by Anna Tsing (2000) in her reflections on global projects, not only moves across space, but changes as it moves, picking up new resonances as it transforms, and is in turn transformed by, new landscapes and people. Luisa, my closest friend at the FANJNH, once told me that permaculture workshops have "a contagious effect," converting enough participants to the practice to ensure the multiplication of knowledge, as those trained, in turn, come to inspire others. As the knowledge of permaculture moved throughout Havana and Cuba, it not only literally changed landscapes and created new subjects (today's Cuban permaculturists) but was also modified and adapted to meet local circumstances, giving rise to a Cuban-inflected variety of permaculture, aptly celebrated in the previously mentioned documentary by Antonio and Rafael and in a FANJNH publication called *Permacultura criolla* (Creole Permaculture; Cruz Hernández, Sánchez Medina, and Cabrera 2006).[3]

The extent to which Cubans have come to recognize their unique contribution to permaculture was evident in the stance taken by many at the 2008 convention. It was clear from several interactions at the meeting that from a Cuban perspective, the knowledge of permaculture no longer resides solely in countries of the so-called global North, like Australia, where it originated, but now lives in Cuba. This position was clear when Pablo publicly stated at the meeting that there was a need to "democratize" official permaculture accreditation practices, criticizing how, at the time, only a few institutions in the global North had the right to endorse the granting of official permaculture diplomas. Pablo, not surprisingly, proposed that institutions in the global South, such as the FANJNH, be granted the same authority in recognition of their proven competence in the field. That this statement came from Pablo, a recipient of the first permaculture classes taught in Cuba and a person who travels overseas several times each year to give talks about the Cuban experience in this area, is significant. On the one hand, his case exemplifies how ideas that circulate globally travel in multiple directions, empowering actors and projects other than those associated with their place of origin; on the other, Pablo's position here also hints at how international recognition and experience shape the way Cubans envision their place within the broader global movement for sustainable urban agriculture and the kinds of claims they feel they have a right to make in an international arena.

Cubans "Who Travel Places" and Image Making

When Pablo first became involved with the FANJNH Permaculture Program, travel opportunities were rare. When the first invitations to travel overseas finally came, Pablo was considered because of his overall competence and his fluency in English. Unlike some government officials who travel with an explicitly political mandate, Pablo always speaks frankly and critically about the challenges his country faces. While a proud Cuban, he never sounds like a mouthpiece for government propaganda. Perhaps for these reasons, as well as for his affable personality and knowledge of sustainable agriculture, he has frequently been invited to participate at international events. The last time I saw him, he proudly told me how he had been granted a passport with "ambassadorial status," meaning he no longer needed to apply for an exit permit every time he traveled overseas. This rare privilege is not surprising considering that Pablo is a great "international ambassador" not only for the FANJNH but also, generally, for Cuba.

For Pablo and other FANJNH employees, involvement in permaculture has meant, among other things, an opportunity to travel overseas—something that, as suggested by Rafael's earlier comment on the Aeroflot couple, is not equally accessible to all Cubans. First, not everyone gets an invitation to travel out of the country for conferences or other types of international exchanges, and, second, having such an invitation does not guarantee that Cuban authorities will grant permission to exit. The possibility of a defection, or of public embarrassment for Cuba, is carefully weighed, and only those considered "trustworthy" receive the opportunity to travel. This trustworthiness, I have been told, is measured in part by the reputation of the Cuban institution that endorses the applicant's request to travel. Workplaces generally take on this responsibility and deal with all aspects of an overseas trip, from purchasing airline tickets to obtaining the necessary visas. In Pablo's case, the institution that took this responsibility was the FANJNH; in the cases of others associated with members of the Department of Urban Agriculture, whom I have known to travel to places like Venezuela, it was the MINAG that took care of such travel requirements.

Over the years, I have noted that travel opportunities for individual FANJNH employees have increased as they have gained global recognition through participation in international conferences, workshops, and urban agriculture networks and as their work has been featured in internationally circulating publications and film documentaries. By 2009, all FANJNH permaculture team members had attended more than one conference and workshop overseas, and a few had even stayed in other countries for long periods as advisors on a variety of urban agriculture programs. Even some producers associated with the FANJNH, like Manolo, had gotten a chance to travel to other countries at the request of event organizers. On a personal level, these experiences represent a chance to purchase material goods not available in Cuba, to see other places, and to make "worldly connections" that might result in friendships and, as already suggested, in future travel opportunities.

Of course, even producers who do not get to travel overseas can still make "worldly connections" and achieve a global presence through their production endeavors, contributing, consciously or not, to shaping the image of Cuban urban agriculture in the world. This, for example, has been the case of producers like Rafael and Jorge, who, while remaining in Cuba, have engaged in "virtual travel," as accounts written by foreign visitors about their patios or parcelas are widely disseminated through websites managed by organizations like *City Farmer* in Canada, *Food First* in the United States, and the Cuba Organic Support Group (COSG) in England. In addition to Internet reporting, patios and parcelas are also featured in a range of documentaries, including a low-budget and modestly distributed film produced within Cuba by Antonio and Rafael; the widely circulated movie *The Power of Community: How Cuba Survived Peak Oil*, made by Faith Morgan in 2006; and the 2007 TV series *The Accidental Revolution*, hosted by the renowned Canadian environmentalist David Suzuki.

That many of these global representations of Cuban urban agriculture showcase gardens like Rafael's in order to deliver the message that people working together can bring about momentous change is, of course, somewhat ironic. Those who create these films or Internet reports rarely stay very long in Cuba and do not appear interested in querying common interpretations of Cuban urban agriculture. Like the Cuban government, the authors of these representations have their own stake in presenting a romanticized idea of Cuban urban agriculture—an idea that continues to fascinate and move those around the world interested in alternative development experiences and in hopeful stories about "the power of community."

The extent to which such romanticized representations, and associated expectations, by "outsiders" shape the way producers and institutional actors within Cuba choose to portray (and develop) their garden work was variously illustrated during my years of research in Havana. As already suggested, the environmental contributions of urban agriculture sites have been increasingly emphasized as environmental sustainability has gained a more prominent position in national and international funding agendas. In my experience, the framing of urban agriculture in environmental terms has been more likely to occur in situations where the producer has felt he or she was addressing an international audience. This was evident, for example, in a 2004 filmed interview I conducted with Vivencio on the commercial herbal garden he cultivated in the central municipality of Plaza. Clearly addressing a broader audience, he started the interview with the following words: "I think it is very appropriate that you came to do this interview with me on this day, the international day of the environment. Much is being said about the environment these days and the need to take care of it because we, the human species, will disappear without it. Here, in this garden we are doing what we can to contribute to this global struggle." He was alluding to a new FANJNH project centered on his garden that involved the composting of kitchen leftovers from neighboring households. Although he was obviously proud of this new program, it seemed strange that he chose to start the interview by emphasizing this aspect of the garden over others I knew had been, and still were, more important to him. The garden, as he had told me earlier, had been created to provide Cubans with "green medicine" at a time when pharmaceutical drugs were scarce. Although Vivencio downplayed the commercial dimension of the garden, I knew from talking to others that herbal gardens were a profitable business in Havana serving a diverse range of customers, including individuals looking for herbs to use in Afro-Cuban rituals that had little to do with physical healing. Whenever I tried to bring up the topic of sales at the garden, Vivencio returned to the social objective of the place and its environmental contribution. His reluctance to share information about sales was no doubt connected to the already-mentioned public disapproval of excessive profit, yet his emphasis on the environment was connected not just to the recent recycling project at his garden but also to his awareness of global trends. The extent to which foreign expectations were seen to guide the activities producers chose to highlight was made patently clear to me in 2002 when Antonio commented on his position on foreigners in relation to his and Rafael's garden project. He stated, "We do not have an explicit agenda to attract foreigners, but foreigners are interested in what is happening with community gardens in Cuba. Our objective is not really to attract foreign visitors but rather to ensure that we secure the resources we need to implement our [environmental and community] projects. Of course, if foreign visitors bring the money we need, then we have to cater to them." Though, as shown in Chapters 5 and 6, it would be unfair to conclude that projects that emphasize the community or the environment are done solely to cater to foreign visitors, foreign funders, or the Cuban government for that matter, it is evident from Antonio's words that such expectations do have an influence on producers. Globally circulating representations of Cuban urban agriculture affect not just the actions of producers within Cuba but also the decisions of many throughout the world who, based on these representations, choose to travel to the island to see and to learn firsthand about the country's urban agriculture experience.

Not Your Average Tourist or Capitalist Entrepreneur

In Special Period Cuba, as mentioned, foreign tourists seeking the Caribbean holiday experience have arrived in ever greater numbers, as have foreign investors entering into joint ventures with the Cuban government. The type of person involved in either case bares little resemblance, in my experience, to the kind of person who chooses to travel to Cuba to collaborate with organizations like the FANJNH. Solidarity with the Cuban revolution or, at the very least, a commitment to alternative development paths appears to be a common denominator of foreign institutions and individuals who, over the years, have helped develop Havana's urban agriculture. In terms of political solidarity, the founders of the Australian Green Team, for example, stated that their original wish had been "to support the socialist state of Cuba after the collapse of the Soviet bloc and the US blockade on trade" (S. Wright et al. 1996). Subsequent Green Team members appeared to share left-leaning political sensibilities, and one of them, I was told, had come from a long line of socialists in Australia. Not every foreigner or foreign institution contributing to the urban agriculture effort in Cuba, of course, has expressed political solidarity with the country. In fact, some organizations have presented their efforts as primarily guided by an apolitical interest in sustainable development in general. Thus, while collaborating with government ministries like the MINAG, the German Agro Acción Alemana, for example, has chosen to present its collaborations as primarily based on a desire to foment a more environmentally sound agriculture in developing nations. In a recent brochure that describes one of its most successful urban agriculture projects in Havana, the AAA underscores this alternative development mandate by commenting on how its mandate is to support small-scale agriculture initiatives on the island that are "close to nature and the consumer" (Deutsche Welthungerhilfe 2001).

Political preferences and official institutional pronouncements aside, those foreigners I met who cooperated with the FANJNH at least initially believed that, in Special Period Cuba, another world was possible. This was the case with Liz, the Australian woman mentioned in Chapter 3, who lived in Havana for several years, assisting the FANJNH with the teaching of permaculture and the organization of garden tours. In her home country, Liz was a committed permaculturist who had worked on a range of social justice projects and who, before joining the Green Team, had participated in a solidarity brigade doing work in the Cuban countryside. Many others had similar trajectories. Among them were Luna, a young environmental activist who participated in an exchange organized between the FANJNH and LifeCycles, an environmental

NGO based in Victoria, Canada; and Martha, a committed social justice and food security activist working at Alternatives in Montreal, Canada. I knew that Liz, and many of the other FANJNH collaborators, gained a critical perspective on Cuba after repeated visits or prolonged stays in the country, yet they did not allow this experience to radically color their subsequent stories of their gardening work in Havana. In fact, subsequent public accounts by foreigners who worked in this field frequently offered celebratory portrayals of the Cuban experience.

Sometimes, these positive representations were the result of political predilections, but more often than not they had to do with personal entanglements and projects. For many of these foreigners, life in Cuba resulted in personal relationships—from friendships to marriages—that indirectly obliged them to retain good relations with hosting institutions that might affect their chances of being welcomed back into the country in the future.[4] For some at least, their agriculture experience in Havana had become a way to claim authority as environmental or alternative development activists once they were back home. The Cuban experience, in this respect, was an important part of these people's professional curricula, used to further them in their chosen career path. This situation was vividly illustrated for me in 2010, as I visited my family in Victoria, Canada. There, in a small neighborhood newsletter, was an article by Luna, whom I had last seen nearly a decade prior in Havana when she was completing her exchange visit with the FANJNH. Her article, which was about her new small business producing organic salad greens, began with her stating how privileged she had been to spend time in Havana so many years ago, learning from Cubans how to grow their own food in the city. Thus, as she burnished her credentials, she simultaneously reinforced the internationally acclaimed image of Cuba as a vanguard country in the field of urban agriculture.

While such representations are based on real experiences and cannot be dismissed out of hand as disingenuous, they constitute at the very least a selective retelling intended to serve personal and institutional projects outside Cuba. Regardless of their purpose, however, such international accounts do show that the experience of Cuban urban agriculture is not just a Cuban story but a global story told by all who, in one way or another, have participated in its making and are personally invested in a certain portrayal of the experience—whether their ultimate goal is change in Cuba or abroad.

Projections for the Future

Back at the Third Permaculture Convention near Havana, looking around at the faces of those making up the international cohort at the meeting, it was difficult for me not to notice that the Cuban delegation was made up of an aging population. In this respect, I had to wonder what the future might hold for permaculture in Cuba. Age aside, however, this was an incredibly resilient group. The FANJNH team was made up of people like Graciela, Pablo, and Luisa who for fifteen years had dedicated countless hours to inspiring other Cubans to take up permaculture. The other institutional representatives present at the meeting, from the president of ACPA to various members of the MINAG, were also faces I had known for over a decade. Most admirable, for me, were the producers who worked on their agricultural projects year after year, against adversities of all kinds. Yet they persisted.

As participants discussed the future of permaculture in Latin America and talked about what they could do to "spread the word," I was transported back to 2001 when I talked to Rodrigo, one of the original founders of the Urban Agriculture Department, right after he had been elected to direct AGUILA, the Latin American Urban Agriculture Network. As he anticipated his upcoming stay in Peru, where AGUILA's headquarters were located, he excitedly told me, "I'm happy because I will remain connected to urban agriculture but now it will not be just through the city [of Havana] but through Latin America. It is a wonderful thing, right? To be able to do something, as a friend of mine says, for the poor of our America while remaining connected to urban agriculture, to be able to transfer all the daring ideas of this city to other cities in the hemisphere!" It was clear that for Rodrigo, as for many of the Cubans present at the 2008 convention, their individual experience with urban agriculture in Cuba connected them with something much bigger that exceeded the frontiers of the nation. From the higher echelons of the Department of Urban Agriculture, made up of individuals well versed in organic food production methods, to the permaculturists employed by the FANJNH, a coherent discourse had emerged that connected post-1989 agricultural experiences in Cuba with global struggles for environmental sustainability and social justice. The leaders of the FANJNH team at the meeting definitely spoke as if they were convinced that everyone there was part of a global struggle against unsustainable development models that had resulted in food insecurity and environmental degradation all over the world. From this perspective, the distinction among permaculture, agro-ecology, and organic agriculture did not seem to matter that much.

Although the 2008 Permaculture Convention was not a political forum for discussing domestic matters, Cubans publicly acknowledged that they were facing their own challenges. The battle to make room for agriculture in the city, so vividly described by General Sio Wong, had not been fully won, and it seemed that urban agriculture was losing ground as parcelas in some areas disappeared to make way for more traditional urban land uses, like housing. Many producers in attendance spoke about the need to continue developing Cuba's alternatives in agricultural production. Among other things, they argued that small-scale production units and practices like intercropping had allowed them to better cope with the three hurricanes that had just hit Cuba. At times like this, when the country was said to have returned, albeit temporarily, to the kind of food scarcity experienced in 1993 (Mesa Lago 2009), the benefits of small-scale, sustainable agriculture were particularly conspicuous.

The FANJNH team, of course, cared about underscoring the benefits of sustainable production technologies, but at the meeting they appeared more concerned with the possibility that Cuba might be going back to the old model of agriculture that Australian Bill Mollison had characterized as directed by a "brown thumb" rather than a green one. Thus, when the topic of chemical fertilizers and pesticides came up, a member of the FANJNH made a public statement that the organization would struggle against a return to this old model. As I listened to this pronouncement, I wondered how the producers present truly felt about this issue. After talking to some of them afterward, I understood that they were not settled on any of these questions. In this respect, I had to wonder where the permaculture movement and sustainable urban agriculture practices in general were headed, and whether global connections, and the global repute of Cuba in this field, would aid in the struggles that had to be fought on the home front.

Conclusion

In 1994, when I first visited Cuba, I could not have imagined that the figure of a screaming pig on the ninth floor of a fancy apartment building in Havana would one day lead me to write this book. Nor could I have thought that this emblematic image would act as a catalyst for an exploration into the social production of urban agriculture sites in Havana, which in turn would propel me to questions of power. As I have argued throughout this book, urban agriculture sites in Havana do not exist outside of power but have, from their inception, been embedded in power relations that extend far beyond the locality. Havana's urban agriculture sites are not autonomous, self-contained, stable, and inert "facts" on the ground that can be simply counted or summarily defined so that one can proceed with the more important job of telling a coherent and seamless story about the evolution of urban agriculture in Cuba. Urban agriculture sites, and especially the parcelas and patios that constitute the primary focus of this exposition, are dynamic and ever-changing products of multiple agents that reflect complex entanglements between the rooted and the mobile, the local and the global, the national and the transnational, the private and the public, the personal and the strictly political in contemporary Cuba. Exploring these entanglements puts into focus the varied agendas and actors involved in the making, remaking, and unmaking of Havana's urban agriculture sites and, ultimately, betters our understanding of the shifting landscapes of power in Special Period Cuba.

As illustrated through ethnographic examples, the official post-1989 shift to urban agriculture in Havana did not just involve the reconfiguration of urban and agricultural landscapes on the island; it opened up a space for public debate on alternative models of development. Some of the issues debated were old, others new. While the desirability of economic incentives to encourage efficiency in agricultural production had been a topic of national deliberation in the past, the talk of a massive and sustained conversion to low-input, small-scale, localized, and organic agriculture in the countryside and the city had no prior precedents. Whether seen to represent an absolute novelty or not, many of the government-endorsed policies and projects that arose at this point were considered to have fundamentally upset the overall direction of past development plans. Initially accepted by many as necessary emergency measures taken to save the country from an imminent debacle, these changes were not equally embraced by all state actors. As suggested by the lively debates reflected in these pages, the Cuban socialist state, like all other states, is not (and has never been) the monolithic, univocal, and unyielding entity so frequently invoked in much of Cuban studies.[1] Urban agriculture and its various associated practices were both contested and defended within, and across, state institutions. In the end, within official circles, continued opposition to urban agriculture and its potential "deviations" reveals deep attachment to modernist development ideals, fear over the loss of bureaucratic power, and a belief that old state projects and ways of operating are better suited to meet the ultimate goals of a socialist society.

In reference to the power wielded by state actors—be they bureaucrats or not—the stories presented here constitute a sort of cautionary tale against an oversimplified reading of the Cuban experience. This book first moves away from an understanding of the state as authoritative, monolithic, all powerful, and coercive and, second, challenges the presumption of an independently rebellious civil society focused on resisting or subverting the designs emanating "from the top." As argued by some authors (e.g., Acanda 1997; Dilla and Oxhorn 2002), civil society and political society in Cuba do not necessarily represent autonomous, or internally homogeneous, spheres of action that exist only in an antagonistic relationship to each other. As attested by several of the cases presented in this book, these two conceptually separate spheres not only are in constant dialogue with each other but at times appear to move in unison. Thus, at least a portion of state employees, state officials, and urban farmers concur on the benefits of small-scale production, on the importance of defending a communitarian ethos, and on the need to address contradictory official policies that, on the one hand, encourage urban agriculture sites to develop in certain directions and, on the other, either curtail these developments or do little to support them. What becomes evident in this analysis is that to understand the role of state actors and producers in the development of urban agriculture sites in Cuba, one must pay attention not just to conflicts that arise between them but to the conversations that take place among them. A focus on cooperation, accommodation, and alliances here is particularly important and leads one to understand that power in Cuba does not rest in the hands of state actors alone. This has been particularly true since the onset of the Special Period, when the state lost much of its prior ability to allocate needed resources to those in charge of implementing state-endorsed programs.

While standard accounts of Cuban urban agriculture to date have primarily emphasized the enabling role of the Cuban state in this field, the account offered in this book not only makes room for the contradictory and less than "enabling acts" of various state institutions and actors but also importantly explores the role played by nonstate actors in this field—from independent producers to national and international NGOs. Nonstate institutions, connected to international donor agencies are shown to have made an important contribution to the development of patios and parcelas in particular. Far from challenging state programs, national and international NGOs working in this field, have largely complemented these programs in a way that has allowed state institutions to retain their ability to direct or redirect the conduct of the population. National and international NGO projects often converge with state initiatives effectively guiding producers, through material and other incentives, toward practices that bring them closer to ideals of agricultural sustainability or community engagement, variously defined. Yet it would be wrong to conclude from these examples that the effectiveness of these initiatives is linked only to the material and symbolic rewards promised, or otherwise delivered, "from above" (whether the above here is conceptualized as the state or the mentioned NGOs).

As I have demonstrated, producers never quite surrender their own personal dreams and agendas, which, as suggested, may or may not be in contradiction with official state pronouncements. While shown to be responsive to the wishes of governmental and nongovernmental organizations working in the field, the producers presented in this book are far from the exemplary docile subjects described in Foucault's (1979) writings. Despite all the constraints producers face, they are remarkably adept at generating their own personal projects and insinuating their own desires onto "the dominant text"—a strategy Certeau (1988, 37) attributes to all those who, ultimately, "must play on and with a terrain imposed . . . and organized by the law of [the other]." Still, such a reading would only partially incorporate the material presented, which also shows that some producers have acquired the power to shape at least "the terrain" in which they work by becoming active participants in the official urban agriculture movement. Here, as argued earlier, Lefebvre's (1998 [1974]) insights, which move away from oversimplified understandings of the power relations involved in the social production of space and encourage empirical study on specific enactments of these relations, are much more promising.

The analysis presented suggests that during the Special Period the encouragement of self-help initiatives, alongside with increased opportunities to connect with the outside world through official linkages with internationally funded NGOs, created new and exciting opportunities for some citizens who, in this way, not only acquired a certain degree of independence from state institutions but also could tap into sources of power previously unavailable to those located at the conceptual margins of the Cuban economy. Here, the connections between individual producers and the international image of Cuba's urban agriculture—an image that the government would like to uphold—cannot be underestimated.

Much has happened in Cuba since I began my research into urban agriculture. Fidel Castro, a pervasive presence in the media in 1997, stepped down in 2006 and now seldom makes public appearances. Raúl Castro, his brother, often described to me as the "godfather" of urban agriculture, has taken over the presidency of Cuba and has implemented a number of reforms that, in some respects, were foreshadowed in the policy changes described in this book that encouraged citizens' self-reliance, private enterprise, modest private profit, and permissible collaborations with nonstate national and international actors.

Although MINAG statistics regarding production outputs in the urban agriculture sector claim that, by 2005, Havana reached the minimum daily supply of fresh vegetables per capita advocated by the Food and Agriculture Organization of the United Nations (Koont 2009), food insecurity remains a problem, as social inequality grows and as Cuba continues to import up to 84 percent of basic food items (Mesa Lago 2009). Taking this national context into account, alongside the global hype about contaminated food sources and environmentally unsustainable food systems, it is no surprise that the development of urban agriculture continues to receive the support of the Cuban government.

As for the small-scale urban farmers I worked with, some have quit and some have passed away. Yet a remarkable majority of them continue on, moved by myriad intermingled motives, including necessity, habit, pride, and just plain enjoyment in what they do. The forms their gardens will take in the future is dependent on multiple factors and actors—not the least of which are producers' own personal commitments and attachments to the spaces they created and nurtured through the years. This commitment was vividly illustrated for me as I briefly stopped in at Rafael's garden in December 2011 and he informed me that, to take advantage of new legislation introduced in connection with the Sixth Cuban Communist Party Congress, he had decided to apply for a business license to establish a tea house in his patio that would be supplied by the herbs grown on site. As I reflected on this announcement, I could not help but note the many transformations undergone in Havana's urban agriculture practices since the early 1990s. From a certain perspective, there seemed to be quite a long distance between the image of a pig illicitly raised for food in an apartment building and the arguably less nutritious fare that might soon be served for a modest fee out of Rafael's patio. Times have no doubt changed, but what remain constant are the flexibility and dynamism of small-scale urban agriculture sites and the ability of producers to continually invent them and reinvent them to adapt to changing circumstances. I feel fortunate to have been allowed into the lives of the producers I met through this research, time after time, to note the changes I record in this book. It is my hope that their stories and those of the production sites they have created and tended can contribute to a more nuanced perspective on urban agriculture in Havana that will be more sensitive to what these sites can reveal about the changing landscapes of power on the island and the ongoing revision of the socialist state project.

Notes

Introduction

1. Cuba is technically an archipelago, but it is commonly referred to as *la isla* (the island) by most Cubans. While many in and outside of Cuba have emphasized the insular character of the country post-1959, as will become evident in the pages that follow, Cuba is a place that has always been constituted through its relationships to other places in what Akhil Gupta and James Ferguson (1992) have rightly described as an always hierarchically organized world. As suggested by the introduction's subtitle, I here draw on Doreen Massey's (2004) work on a global sense of place that works with a nonessentialist definition of place as internally diverse and resulting from relationships that spread outward beyond the locality.

2. The work of Eckstein (2004) on migration as well as that of the Cuban economist Pedro Monreal on the exportation of Cuban experts (cited in García Quiñones 2001) vividly illustrates the contributions that these worldly connections and their associated remittances have made to the Cuban economy.

3. The phrase *la revolución* is commonly used in Cuba to refer to the societal changes that began on January 1, 1959, when the leaders of the 26th of July Movement came to power after overthrowing the dictator Fulgencio Batista. I will henceforth adhere to this usage of the phrase.

4. Although publications in this area abound, I have found the perspectives of some authors particularly relevant to my own work. These include Ariana Hernández-Reguant's (2004) arguments on shifting perspectives on the communitarian ethos in the culture industry, Sean Brotherton's (2008) analysis of the rise of hybrid subjectivities and changing statecraft in the health service sector, and Adrian Hearn's (2008) description of reconfigured state projects in the field of community development.

5. I here use the term *urban agriculture* as it was used in the early 1990s in Cuba, to refer solely to primary food production activities in the city. My emphasis on edible products here departs from more encompassing definitions of urban agriculture that include the production of nonedible products, such as ornamental plants, for commercialization purposes (United Nations

Development Programme 1996). Although a similarly comprehensive definition is also used at present in the Cuban context, I have chosen to retain the initial definition because it still reflects the way in which the majority of those I work with use the term.

6. It should be noted that the term *parcela* is used in the agriculture sector to refer to individual plots of land but in the urban agriculture field the term denotes a small garden located on public land.

7. Organoponic gardens consist of compost-filled, raised beds with a few lines of drip irrigation that make cultivation possible on sites with unsuitable or no soil.

8. Unless a published source is identified, citations like this one were drawn from interviews or taped group meetings that took place in Spanish and were later transcribed and translated by the author.

9. These headlines were featured in a number of different magazines and newspapers written by different journalists between 1991 and 1992 (Bedriñana Isart 1991, 1992; Gumá 1992; Mayoral 1992; Shelton 1992a, 1992b).

10. Although, as noted in Table 1, there are two types of organoponic gardens: the high-yield organoponics (*organopónicos de alto rendimiento*, OAR) and the Popular organoponics (*organopónicos populares*), henceforth, I will follow common usage and use the general term *organopónico* to refer only to the OARs.

11. Their ages ranged from thirty-five to ninety, with thirty (71 percent) of them over age fifty-five. The predominance of men and older people in this sample is usually reported as the demographic norm among small-scale urban farmers in Havana (Murphy 1999; Cruz Hernández and Sánchez Medina 2001).

12. In my analysis of the information collected, I used qualitative data software to assist me in identifying the variables that might account for significant differences in perspective. Included here were factors such as gender, age, level of education, employment status, current occupation, form of involvement in urban agriculture (e.g., producer or service provider), formal institutional affiliation, and land tenure status over related production sites (private versus usufruct). Only those variables directly addressed in the chapters were found to be significant to the questions guiding this book.

13. The U.S. dollar was withdrawn from circulation in 2004 and replaced by the equivalent Cuban currency known as the *peso convertible*, to be distinguished from the still circulating *peso cubano* (Cuban peso). Although some commercially oriented urban agriculture sites did sell part of their production outputs to the tourist industry in hard currency equivalents, these transactions were still the exception within the sector at the time of research.

14. Experimentation with more decentralized forms of economic and political decision making had already begun prior to 1989, driven in part by the official recognition of inefficiencies fomented by a strongly centralized system (García

Pleyán 1996; Amuchastegui 1999). Still, the crisis of the late 1980s greatly sped up the pace of such experimentation.

15. Here I am alluding to the work of Aradhana Sharma and Akhil Gupta (2006, 25), who argue that in a transnational world, the state is "but one node . . . in a horizontal network of institutions and individuals through which power is exercised, and not the vertically higher institution in which power inheres."

Chapter 1

1. When referring to public figures whose opinions are part of the public record, I first give the true proper name and then, following common usage in Cuba, use only the first name or nickname of the person in question. Although there are exceptions to this usage, I incorporate it into my writing because I feel it reveals a very different conceptualization of those in positions of power within Cuba (at least at the rhetorical level). To ensure anonymity, all other individuals cited in the text are referred to only by pseudonyms.

2. In 1968, in what came to be known as the Revolutionary Offensive, retail businesses of all kinds were absorbed into the state sector.

3. Although in some respects the ration could be said to have instilled in resident Cubans the feeling of partaking in what David Bell and Gil Valentine (1997, 169), referring to national culinary traditions, have called a "feast of imagined commensality," in the Cuban context, where shortages were the norm in revolutionary times, the word *feast* acquires ironic resonance.

4. The First Agrarian Reform, launched in 1959, gave land title to approximately 110,000 peasants; it also transferred 44 percent of agricultural land—in the form of large landholdings—to the state. The Second Agrarian Reform, carried out in 1963, further raised the percentage of state-owned and managed agricultural land to 63 percent.

5. For an account of how farmers in the countryside perceive these changes, see the work of Maria Gropas (2006).

6. The original Spanish lyrics are *El que siembra su maíz que se coma su pilón.*

Chapter 2

1. This law, which violates international trade laws, attempts to curtail Cuban trade relations with other countries in a number of ways. For example, it allows U.S. companies to sue foreign companies that conduct business with Cuba involving property previously "confiscated" by the Cuban government from U.S. citizens. Moreover, it forbids the executives of companies working in Cuba and their families from entering the United States.

2. It should be noted that in 1999, the U.S. government approved an agricultural waiver of the embargo, allowing U.S. farmers to export some agricultural items,

like grains and chicken, to Cuba. In 2000, the sale of these items to Cuba was authorized by the U.S. government on a case-by-case basis. By 2003, such authorizations had resulted in profits of $282 million for the U.S. farm sector (Marquis 2003). According to Emily Morris (2008, 788), however, the U.S. share of Cuba's imports fell from 7 to 5 percent between 2003 and 2006, when China and Venezuela became major investors as well as key sources of imports for Cuba.

3. These well-documented acts of warfare have, over the years, affected animals like pigs, bees, cows, chickens, and rabbits as well as crops like sugar cane, coffee, tobacco, plantains, and citrus trees (Hinckle and Turner 1981; Herman 1982; Smith 1987; Paterson 1994; Blum 2000).

4. Quotations from this and all other meetings that I was authorized to tape are taken verbatim from resulting transcripts. As indicated earlier, only renowned public figures are mentioned by name.

5. Of course, the association of food production gardens with the act of military defense in times of national crisis is not unique to Cuba, having been noted also in descriptions of the so-called victory gardens associated with World War I and World War II in various parts of the world, including the United States, England, and Australia. For specific examples, see Bentley (1998, 114), Crouch and Ward (1988, 72), Dickson Wright (2000, 222–24), Symons (1982, 164), and Warner and Durlach (1987, 17).

6. Raúl here was likely referring to a program known as Plan Turquino, which in the late 1980s, made agricultural work obligatory for young men finishing their military service (Rosset and Benjamin 1994, 70).

7. The sale of seeds and technical literature falls under the category of protected items, and these products have "low ceilings" (ranging from 10 to 25 percent of the wholesale price) on price markups.

8. Resolution 75, promulgated by the government of Havana, stipulated that the prices for products sold at organopónicos should be 20 percent below those of the nearest agricultural market (*agromercado*) yet there were reports that this was not always respected. Likewise, while high-yield organopónicos were created specifically to meet the food needs of local residents, by 2000, much to the dismay of the general public, five of the seventeen high-yield organopónicos (OARs) in the city sought, and were granted, legal authorization to sell to the tourist sector (Cruz Hernández and Sánchez Medina 2001, 44).

9. The exploitation of one individual by another was explicitly banned in Article 14 of the amended 1992 Cuban Constitution.

10. Even though organopónicos are associated with controversial "openings," such as the linkage of profit to productivity, they are easier to control being less numerous and more closely integrated into the state's regulatory apparatus.

11. Horticulturalist Clubs, which numbered 850 in the city of Havana by 2002, are voluntary organizations that bring together urban farmers working in the same neighborhood. These associations are independent in that they are not subordinated to any institutions, yet they do not have the legal right to administer funds. The landholdings of those belonging to a horticulturalist club are entered into the municipal land registry. The groups facilitate the educational work of agricultural extension workers and also act as channels for material incentives given out by various institutions to producers.

12. It should be noted that prior to the Special Period, there were already experiments under way to increase citizens' participation in decision making in Havana and Cuba in general. The 1986 Party Program stated, "The increasing conscious participation of the people is the decisive factor in the construction of socialism" (quoted in García Pleyán 1996, 185). The Neighborhood Transformation Workshops, created in 1988 under the guidance of GDIC, were an attempt to encourage such participation and were instrumental in the creation of the most localized instance of government in Havana: the Popular Councils (*consejos populares*). Unfortunately, although intended to effect a "democratization" of Cuba's political system, these government organs, much like the CDR and the FMC, became little more than "conveyor belts" for the transfer of information between various levels of government (Dilla 1996).

13. According to my review of media coverage, the term *Jefe de Área* was used from 1991 to 1994.

14. The phrase "fifth column" originated in the Spanish Civil War and is used to refer to a minority within a country that conspires with foreign forces to undermine a national struggle.

15. This position on self-employment has since been radically reversed, with the government of Raúl Castro granting numerous self-employment permits in 2011.

Chapter 3

1. The Cuban economist Pedro Monreal comments on the economic import of remittances associated with unprecedented migration during this time by stating that "the exportation of workers [through the migration of highly educated individuals] is one of the areas with the most 'competitive advantages' for the country and in fact a significant section of the Cuban economy's 'modern' sector is outside its formal borders" (quoted in García Quiñones 2001).

2. I am referring here to a range of authors (Rosset and Benjamin 1994; Murphy 1999; Companioni et al. 2002; J. Wright 2009) who, while contributing important and insightful analyses of urban agriculture in Cuba, remain too focused on a macro perspective.

3. By 1997, Havana had been able to recuperate only half of its previous public transportation capacity. Private and state taxis circulated widely in Havana, but their fares were inaccessible to the average citizen without access to dollars (the cheapest fare for a local group taxi with a fixed route amounted to 10 Cuban pesos per person, exorbitant for those earning an average monthly salary of 170 pesos).

4. By 1997, one million bicycles had been sold by the government at affordable prices to prioritized users—workers and students—but spare parts were difficult to find once they were needed (González Sedeño 1997).

5. Only about a third of the producers interviewed (fifteen out of the forty-two) were engaged in full-time employment at the time of the research; the rest were officially retired (twenty), were self-employed (three), or were housewives with no previous connection to the formal workforce (four).

6. Whereas before comparable goods had been available in pesos at subsidized prices through state ration stores or the parallel state market, now they were primarily sold, with a markup of 140 percent, through state dollar stores. In 1997, three years after they were first opened, dollar stores contributed two-thirds of the state's total currency income (Eckstein 2004, 320), which, in theory, was invested in social programs that would benefit the entire population.

7. The use of gardening to express individual or household identity has been noted in various parts of the world (e.g., Mukerji 1990; Chevalier 1998; Rotenberg 1999).

8. The teaching of permaculture advocates, among other things, the creation of agricultural systems that imitate "nature's design" by replicating the multilevel style of vegetation found in forested areas.

9. According to an account I collected from Rogelio, one of the founders of the Urban Agriculture Department in Havana, I knew this was not the first time Ina's garden had fallen under the radar of pertinent state officials. As we spoke about gardens in core municipalities of the city, Rogelio candidly told me how, only a year prior, his office had been contacted by the female caretaker of a garden in Centro Habana (the description fit Ina's garden) to enlist the department's help in fighting a planned construction project on the site. He added, "I honestly did not know that plot existed. That was a real discovery. Who would have thought it would be possible in that area!"

Chapter 4

1. José Martí is a Cuban national hero who fought for Cuba's independence in colonial times. Ever since Fidel acknowledged José Martí to have been the intellectual leader of the 1950s Cuban revolution, the words of Martí have been given the status of incontestable wisdom.

2. The importance of "socialist ownership of all the people over the means of production"—a proprietorship understood to be exercised via state institutions for the benefit of all—was inscribed in Article 14 of the 1976 Constitution and was thought to be an essential component of the socialist organization of the Cuban economy.

3. In the other cases I knew where separate claims over a parcela site had been put forward by other members of the community after the site had been cleared and brought under production, the right of the parceleros was also reasserted at least in part by invoking the personal effort invested in converting a previous "wasteland" into a useful and "productive" site.

4. This garden was created in 1996. Most of the neighbors involved in the project were in their senior years. Pedro and Román were in their late fifties; Gabriela and Fulgencio were over sixty. Ruth, the remaining neighbor in charge of a plot, was a single mother of two children in her forties.

5. In only one of the usufruct-land gardens considered in this study (Ina's garden mentioned in the previous chapter) were people other than the producers involved in the clearing of the land as two men were hired to help clean the site.

6. This official position, of course, was to change in 2010 when Raúl Castro, praising the advantages of private production, introduced a series of agricultural reforms that further decentralized the agriculture sector.

7. With "everything from the state," I am alluding to the 1979 speech by Fidel Castro cited in Chapter 1 (in García Pleyán 1996, 186).

8. Here, Manolo is referring to the much celebrated inauguration of a statue of John Lennon in one of the city plazas in the well-to-do municipality of El Vedado.

9. Tellingly, in a pre–Special Period ethnography, Mona Rosendahl (1997, 158) pointed out that one way in which state power makes itself felt in Cuba is precisely through the knowledge "that power can be exercised erratically and incomprehensibly."

10. For information on the ways in which the MINAG has facilitated the sharing and dissemination of knowledge based on farmers' own experiences, see Rosset and Benjamin (1994, 76–77).

Chapter 5

1. Intercropping involves maximizing the use of a space by planting together complementary crops that do not compete for the same resources.

2. I was told that those parcelas that were successful in terms of outputs and were authorized to commercialize their products were "defended" by the MINAG for the contribution they made to the population's overall food security.

3. This Taller de Renovación de Barrio (TRB) was fashioned after the Talleres de Transformación de Barrio (TTB), initiated throughout the city prior to the

Special Period by the Grupo de Desarrollo Integral de la Capital (GDIC) to encourage participatory planning. TTBs receive logistical and other support from GDIC.

4. It should be noted that housing was identified as the number one need, while recreation and green spaces were ranked third and fourth, respectively, in importance by those who participated in the community workshops.

5. About the opposition to the garden, I was told, "Remember, we are talking about an area that could be inhabited by many. Imagine how many people could be accommodated in an area that is twenty-five and a half meters in width and about fifteen meters in length. That lot is highly valued as residential land and also as real estate, at the level of business investment. Land in this area [Habana Vieja] is highly valued."

6. Adrian Hearn (2008) discusses an earlier episode involving Jorge's garden when the Office of the Historian allegedly prioritized support for a dance troupe over a garden-related project that, according to the author, held more promise for the well-being of the community. Hearn's argument that the garden project, which involved disseminating Afro-Cuban medicinal knowledge, was not given support because the dance troupe held more revenue-generating promise for the Office of the Historian is contradicted by my own ethnographic data. On my last visit to Havana on December 2011, the garden site was still standing, whereas the community space created for the Afro-Cuban dance troupe had been abandoned.

7. Everyone in the group knew of my research project and was happy to cooperate with me. They also asked for my assistance with certain tasks that included phoning people to remind them of meeting times, taking meeting notes, and assisting in the reproduction of the only brochure produced by the group.

8. The Taller could dedicate only a small portion of its regular budget to projects related to the environment, but it was authorized to apply for third-party sources of funding for the project through the Office of the Historian.

9. The raising of pigs is officially authorized in only a few areas in the outskirts of the city.

10. Although on occasion these visits, particularly when involving foreigners, involved donated volunteer labor from the visitors, who also left behind tools and sometimes even gave a bit of money for Jorge's wife to cook a meal for everyone, in the end they represented more of a drain than a support in Jorge's life.

11. Even though the Taller here appropriated Jorge's work claiming it as its own, Juliana generally criticized other institutions that counted Jorge's gardens as part of their programs. Talking about how the garden had been counted as part of the CDR-MINAG Patio and Parcela Movement, she complained, "They don't

know or understand the project. It is not that they do not know we exist. They even speak about us. They just assume that we are part of them, as if by the grace of God, and this is wrong." Similarly, Luis, an employee of the FANJNH, which also counted Jorge's garden as its own, negatively commented on this institutional tendency to appropriate Jorge's work, saying, "Jorge is in a position where everyone exerts influence over him; everyone wants to receive a prize for the work done in the garden, even when they contribute nothing toward it."

12. The TRB's primary objective, reproduced in its official brochure, includes "the improvement of the quality of life of neighborhood inhabitants through the preservation of tangible and intangible values."

13. Note that even the gardeners on Dawn Street in defending their garden lots from potential construction had invoked the way they had contributed to the community by cleaning the site. In other cases I knew where a parcela had come under attack, besides underscoring the contribution made to the community by cleaning up the site, those producers involved made the point that they often share produce with members of the broader community free of charge. Thus, in the case of the parcela Ina and other women had initiated in Centro Habana, the right to the parcela had been defended against a competing claim for a factory renovation by arguing that the factory would do nothing good or "productive" with the site except use it as a parking lot for loading and unloading merchandise. Ina and the other gardeners, on the other hand, made the point that they had turned the site into "the garden of the neighborhood," sharing herbs produced there with other neighbors free of charge.

14. He was referring to the 1997 Cuban *ley del medioambiente* (environmental law).

Chapter 6

1. According to an official count, by 2000, El Cerro had 424 parcelas while Habana Vieja had only 39. While I was unable to find statistics for productive patios in Habana Vieja, I was told that they were not numerous and could hardly compare to the 905 patios counted in El Cerro.

2. While the MINAG encourages the existence in any garden of as many subprograms as may be practical in a given environment, the official position of high-level ministry officials is that quality matters more than quantity. Thus, Adolfo Nodals, president of the National Urban Agriculture Department, publicly proclaimed at the 2001 Annual Meeting of Patios and Parcelas that the creation of model gardens "is not a matter of mechanically applying subprograms" and that "it is not the number of subprograms present, but the quality and health of crops and animals under production that counts." During an interview, Evelio González, the director of the Agricultural Inputs and Service Stores, reiterated this notion as he emphatically stated, "Gardens are first

selected at the base, taking into account the most obvious criteria: production should meet the requirements associated with a given type of crop. We do not care if there be one, two, or three crops represented. Rather, what is important to us is that what is produced be in optimal condition, superior to those found in the case of other producers within the same area. . . . Quality is what matters."

3. There were other important differences in the models of agriculture promoted by the FANJNH and the MINAG. Lower-level MINAG employees in their selection of gardens also emphasized what they described as *sanidad* (hygiene) in the production site. By hygiene, they often meant proper weeding, which was something the FANJNH advised against for a number of different reasons, including the prevention of soil erosion and pest control.

4. The cleaning up of the garden under Rafael's directions involved hiding "messy" yucca shoots, removing dried up plants, moving lettuce plants from one spot to another, and tidying up his compost pile. This, as he understood it, was done to meet the requirement for "health" and "hygiene," verbally communicated to him by the local ministry representative.

5. Within a year of its inception, the movement had incorporated nearly 70,000 patios and parcelas throughout Havana—an impressive increase over the nearly 8,000 initially registered with the Ministerio de la Agricultura. Of these 70,000 sites, 159 were granted the title of model sites at the level of each city district. From this group came the "models" for each municipality and, subsequently, for the city as a whole.

6. Hearn (2008, 114–19) details some of the bureaucratic obstacles experienced by the PCCA to receive foreign assistance.

Chapter 7

1. Elsewhere, I discuss the importance of this financial assistance to Manolo and the manner in which it influenced the development of his production site (Premat 2009).

2. ACAO originated in 1993 when a group of Cuban agricultural professionals, who believed in the superiority of organic farming, created an association to educate farmers and pertinent institutions about organic methods of production. This group received the Right to Livelihood Award (Alternative Nobel Prize) in 1999.

3. It is not my intention here to suggest that there was no other circulating knowledge on sustainable agriculture in the country. Indeed, there was, as evidenced by the earlier mention of ACAO.

4. These personal relationships affected the urban agriculture field beyond what I can detail here. Thus, Liz's marriage to a Cuban, for example, translated into her

extending her stay in Havana, as well as her cooperation with the FANJNH's permaculture projects. On the other side of the equation, Antonio's departure from Cuba in 2006 with a U.S. girlfriend he met through his urban agriculture work left a void for Jorge's wife, who felt his departure, along with Juliana's, marked the end of Jorge's parcela as she knew it.

Conclusion

1. I am here drawing on an extensive literature that queries the social construction of the state as a homogeneous entity with a coherent, unified project (see Abrams 1988; Mitchell 1991; Gupta 1995; Ferguson and Gupta 2002).

References

Abrams, P. (1988). "Notes on the difficulty of studying the state." *Journal of Historical Sociology* 1(1):58–89.

Acanda, J. L. (1997). "Releyendo a Gramsci: Hegemonía y sociedad civil." *Temas* 10 (April–June):75–86.

Acosta, D. (2002). "Cuba: Pigs out of Havana, orders Castro." *Inter Press Service.* Retrieved October 2002 from *www.ips.org/institutional.*

Amuchastegui, D. (1999). *Cuba's armed forces: Power and reforms.* Paper presented at the Eighth Annual Meeting of the Association for the Study of the Cuban Economy (ASCE), Coral Gables, Florida, August 12–14.

Amuchastegui, D. (2000). *Far: Mastering reforms.* Paper presented at the Ninth Annual Meeting of the Association for the Study of the Cuban Economy (ASCE), Coral Gables, Florida, August 5.

Anderson, B. (1991). *Imagined communities: Reflections on the origin and spread of nationalism.* London: Verso.

Anderson, J. L. (1997). *Che: A revolutionary life.* New York: Grove Press.

Anonymous. (1967). "La Habana se desburocratiza." *Bohemia,* March 4, 1.

Appadurai, A. (1988a). "Introduction: Place and voice in anthropological theory." *Cultural Anthropology* 3(1):16–20.

Appadurai, A. (1988b). "Putting hierarchy in its place." *Cultural Anthropology* 3(1):36–49.

Appadurai, A. (1990). "Disjuncture and difference in the global economy." *Public Culture* 2(2):1–24.

Bedriñana Isart, S. (1991). "Los huertos populares avanzan a paso de gigante." *Tribuna de La Habana,* December 23.

Bedriñana Isart, S. (1992). "Sembrando voluntad: Capital de los huertos." *Tribuna de La Habana,* March 22.

Bedriñana Isart, S. (1996). "El verde encuentra su horizonte." *Tribuna de La Habana,* November 3.

Bell, D., and G. Valentine. (1997). *Consuming geographies: We are where we eat.* London: Routledge.

Benjamin, M., J. Collins, and M. Scott. (1986). *No free lunch: Food and revolution in Cuba today.* New York: Grove Press.

Bentley, A. (1998). *Eating for victory: Food rationing and the politics of domesticity.* Urbana: University of Illinois Press.

Blum, W. (2000). *Rogue state: A guide to the world's only superpower.* Monroe, ME: Common Courage Press.

Boorstein, E. (1968). *The economic transformation of Cuba: A first-hand account.* New York: Modern Reader Paperbacks.

Bourdieu, P. (1977). *Outline of a theory of practice.* Cambridge: Cambridge University Press.

Brotherton, P. S. (2008). "'We have to think like capitalists but continue being socialists': Medicalized subjectivities, emergent capital, and socialist entrepreneurs in post-Soviet Cuba." *American Ethnologist* 35(2):259–74.

Burchardt, H. J. (2000). *La última reforma agraria del siglo: La agricultura cubana entre el cambio y el estancamiento.* Caracas: Editorial Nueva Sociedad.

Butterworth, D. (1980). *The people of Buena Ventura: Relocation of slum dwellers in postrevolutionary Cuba.* Urbana: University of Illinois Press.

Castro Medel, O. (2001). "Un niño sembró un corazón." *Juventud Rebelde*, July 17.

Castro Ruz, F. (1993). *La historia me absolverá: Edición anotada.* Havana: Oficina de Publicaciones del Consejo de Estado.

Castro Ruz, R. (1994a). "It can be done." *Granma International* 29 (31/32):8.

Castro Ruz, R. (1994b). "Speech given by Raúl Castro." *Granma International*, August 17.

Certeau, M. de. (1988). *The practice of everyday life.* Berkeley: University of California Press.

Chevalier, S. (1998). "From woolen carpet to grass carpet: Bridging house and garden in an English suburb." In *Material cultures: Why some things matter*, edited by D. Miller, 47–71. Chicago: University of Chicago Press.

Chong, I. (1991). "Del balcón a la cocina." *Juventud Rebelde*, November 24.

Companioni, N., Y. Ojeda Hernández, E. Páez, and C. Murphy. (2002). "The growth of urban agriculture." In *Sustainable agriculture and resistance: Transforming food production in Cuba*, edited by F. Funes, G. Luis, M. Bourque, N. Pérez, and P. Rosset, 220–36. Oakland, CA: Food First Books.

Corrales, J. (2004). "The gatekeeper state: Limited reforms and regime survival in Cuba, 1989–2002." *Latin American Research Review* 39(2):35–65.

Crouch, D., and C. Ward. (1988). *The allotment: Its landscape and culture.* London: Faber.

Cruz Hernández, M. C., and Y. Murciano. (1996). "La mujer en la agricultura urbana: Apuntes sobre una experiencia cubana." Unpublished manuscript.

Cruz Hernández, M. C., and R. Sánchez Medina. (2001). *Agricultura y ciudad: Una*

References

clave para la sustentabilidad. Havana: Fundación Antonio Núñez Jiménez de la Naturaleza el Hombre.

Cruz Hernández, M. C., R. Sánchez Medina, and C. Cabrera, eds. (2006). *Permacultura criolla.* Havana: Fundación Antonio Núñez Jiménez de la Naturaleza y el Hombre.

Dean, M. (1999). *Governmentality: Power and the rule in modern society.* Thousand Oaks, CA: Sage Publications.

Deutsche Welthungerhilfe. (2001). "Organopónico vivero alamar: A little success story of development cooperation. Havana." Retrieved November 2011 from *www.welthungerhilfe.de/projects-cuba.html.*

Díaz Vázquez, J. (2000). "Consumo y distribución normada de alimentos y otros bienes en Cuba." In *La última reforma agraria del siglo: La agricultura cubana entre el cambio y el estancamiento,* edited by H.-J. Burchardt, 33–56. Caracas: Nueva Sociedad.

Dickson Wright, C. (2000). *Food: What we eat and how we eat; a twentieth century anthology.* London: Elan Press.

Dilla, H., ed. (1996). *La participación en Cuba y los retos del futuro.* Havana: Centro de Estudios sobre América (CEA).

Dilla, H., A. Fernández Soriano, and M. Castro Flores. (1997). *Movimientos barriales en cuba: Un análisis comparativo.* San Salvador: FUNDE.

Dilla, H., and P. Oxhorn. (2002). "The virtues and misfortunes of civil society in Cuba." *Latin American Perspectives* 29(4):11–30.

Dirección Provincial de Planificación Física y Arquitectura Ciudad Habana. (1984). *Plan director ciudad de La Habana.* Havana: Instituto Cubano de Geodesia y Cartografía.

Dumont, R. (1970). *Cuba: Socialism and development.* New York: Grove Press.

Eckstein, S. (1994). *Back from the future: Cuba under Castro.* Princeton, NJ: Princeton University Press.

Eckstein, S. (2004). "Dollarization and its discontents: Remittances and the remaking of Cuba in the post-Soviet era." *Comparative Politics* 36(3):313–30.

Fenderson, A. (2004). "Peak oil and permaculture: David Holmgren on energy descent." Post Carbon Institute. Retrieved January 2012 from *www.energybulletin.net/node/524.*

Ferguson, J., and A. Gupta. (2002). "Spatializing states: Toward an ethnography of neoliberal governmentality." *American Ethnologist* 29(4):981–1002.

Fernández Soriano, A. (1997). "Movimientos comunitarios, participación y medio ambiente." *Temas* 9 (January–March): 26–32.

Fernández Soriano, A. (1999). "Realidades, retos y posibilidades de los municipios en el fin de siglo." In *Gobiernos de izquierda en América Latina: El desafío del cambio,* edited by B. Stolowicz, 165–82. Mexico City: Plaza y Valdés Editores.

Fernández Soriano, A. (2001). "Las ongs en Cuba." Personal communication.

Fernández Soriano, A., and R. Otazo Conde. (1996). "Comunidad, autogestión y medio ambiente." In *La participación en Cuba y los retos del futuro*, edited by H. Dilla, 225–37. Havana: Centro de Estudios Sobre América (CEA).

Foucault, M. (1979). *Discipline and punish: The birth of the prison*. New York: Vintage Books.

Foucault, M. (1980). "Truth and power." In *Power and knowledge: Selected interviews and other writings, 1972–1977*, edited by C. Gordon, 109–33. New York: Pantheon.

Foucault, M. (1991). "Governmentality." In *The Foucault effect: Studies in governmentality*, edited by G. Burchell, C. Gordon, and P. Miller, 87–105. Chicago: University of Chicago Press.

García Pleyán, C. (1996). "Participación y decentralización en el planeamiento territorial." In *La participación en Cuba y los retos del futuro*, edited by H. Dilla, 184–94. Havana: Centro de Estudios Sobre América (CEA).

García Quiñones, C. (2001). "International migrations in Cuba: Persisting trends and changes." Retrieved November 2003 from *lanic.utexas.edu/project/asce/pdfs*.

González Sedeño, M. (1997). "Un transporte alternativo en La Habana: La bicicleta." In *Quiénes hacen ciudad? Ambiente y participación popular: Cuba, Puerto Rico, República Dominicana*, edited by L. Camacho, 202–16. Cuenca, Ecuador: SIAP.

Gramsci, A. (1971). *Selections from the prison notebooks*. New York: International Publishers.

Gropas, M. (2006). "Landscape, revolution and property regimes in rural Havana." *Journal of Peasant Studies* 33(2):248–77.

Gumá, G. (1992). "Avanza la siembra en solares capitalinos." *Granma*, March 20.

Gupta, A. (1995). "Blurred boundaries: The discourse of corruption, the culture of politics, and the imagined state." *American Ethnologist* 22(2):375–402.

Gupta, A., and J. Ferguson. (1992). "Beyond 'culture': Space, identity, and the politics of difference." *Cultural Anthropology* 7(1):6–23.

Hearn, A. (2008). *Religion, social capital, and development*. Durham, NC: Duke University Press.

Herman, E. S. (1982). *The real terror network: Terrorism in fact and propaganda*. Boston: South End Press.

Hernández-Reguant, A. (2004). "Copyrighting Che: Art and authorship under Cuban late socialism." *Public Culture* 16(1):1–29.

Hinckle, W., and W. W. Turner. (1981). *The fish is red: The story of the secret war against Castro*. New York: Harper and Row.

Hoffman, B. (2000). "La economía política de la crisis y transformación en Cuba." In *La última reforma agraria del siglo: La agricultura cubana entre el cambio y el estancamiento*, edited by H.-J. Burchardt, 59–70. Caracas: Nueva Sociedad.

Instituto Cubano de Radio y Televisión. (1993). "Huertos populares" (Television broadcast, Tape MT1020). *Tierra, Sol y Algo Más*. Havana, December 26.

Kapcia, A. (2008). "Does Cuba fit yet or is it still 'exceptional'?" *Journal of Latin American Studies* 40(4):627–50.

Koont, S. (2009). "The urban agriculture of Havana." *Monthly Review* 60(8):1–14.

Li, T. (2005). "Beyond 'the state' and failed schemes." *American Anthropologist* 107(3):383–93.

Li, T. (2007). *The will to improve: Governmentality, development, and the practice of politics.* Durham, NC: Duke University Press.

Lefebvre, H. (1998 [1974]). *The production of space.* Oxford: Blackwell.

Marquis, C. (2003). "Senate approves easing of curbs on Cuba travel." *New York Times*, October 24.

Massey, D. (2004). "Geographies of responsibility." *Geografiska Annaler: Series B, Human Geography* 86(1):5–18.

Mayoral, M. J. (1992). "Crecen los huertos populares." *Granma*, January 28.

Mesa Lago, C. (2009). "La economía de Cuba hoy: Retos internos y externos." *Desarrollo Económico* 49(195):421–50.

Mitchell, T. (1991). "The limits of the state: Beyond statist approaches and their critics." *American Political Science Review* 85(1):77–96.

Morris, E. (2008). "Cuba's new relationship with foreign capital: Economic policy-making since 1990." *Journal of Latin American Studies* 40(4):769–92.

Mukerji, C. (1990). "Reading and writing with nature: Social claims and the French formal garden." *Theory and Society* 19(6):651–79.

Murphy, C. (1999). *Cultivating Havana: Urban agriculture and food security in the years of crisis.* Oakland, CA: Food First, Institute of Food and Development Policy.

North American Congress on Latin America. (1995). "Cuba: Adapting to a post-Soviet world." *NACLA Report on the Americas* 29(2):6–46.

Pages, R. (1991). "Y crecieron los huertos y parcelas." *Tribuna de La Habana*, July 3.

Pages, R. (1997a). "Organopónicos en la capital: No desacreditar una alternativa valiosa." *Granma*, March 6.

Pages, R. (1997b). "Tenemos que desatar todo lo que limita el desarrollo de las fuerzas productivas." *Granma*, December 30.

Paterson, T. G. (1994). *Contesting Castro: The United States and the triumph of the Cuban revolution.* New York: Oxford University Press.

Pelayo, T. (1995). "Contribución de ONG a los huertos populares." *Tribuna de La Habana*, July 6.

Premat, A. (1998). "Feeding the self and cultivating identities in Havana, Cuba." Master's thesis, York University, Toronto.

Premat, A. (2009). "State power, private plots and the greening of Havana's urban agriculture movement." *City and Society* 21(1):28–57.

Rodríguez, M., and Y. Ferrán. (1996). "Organopónicos de alto rendimiento: Un reto a la eficiencia." *Tribuna de La Habana*, August 4.

Rodriguez Calderón, M. (1995). "El huerto de Pastorita." *Bohemia*, September 29, 18–19.

Rosendahl, M. (1997). *Inside the revolution: Everyday life in socialist Cuba.* Ithaca, NY: Cornell University Press.

Rosset, P., and M. Benjamin. (1994). *The greening of the revolution: Cuba's experiment with organic agriculture.* Sydney: Ocean Press.

Rotenberg, R. (1999). "Landscape and power in Vienna: Gardens of discovery." In *Theorizing the city: The new urban anthropology reader*, edited by L. Setha, 138–68. New Brunswick, NJ: Rutgers University Press.

Schweid, R. (2004). *Che's Chevrolet, Fidel's Oldsmobile: On the road in Cuba.* Chapel Hill: University of North Carolina Press.

Scarpaci, J., M. Coyula, and R. Segre. (1997). *Havana: Two faces of the Antillean metropolis.* New York: Wiley.

Scott, J. C. (1998). *Seeing like a state: How certain schemes to improve the human condition have failed.* New Haven, CT: Yale University Press.

Sharma, A., and A. Gupta. (2006). *The anthropology of the state: A reader.* Malden, MA: Blackwell.

Shelton, A. (1992a). "Sembrando el 60% de los solares yermos destinados a huertos populares." *Granma*, February 6.

Shelton, A. (1992b). "Siembra popular: Un quehacer en desarrollo." *Granma*, February 8.

Smith, W. S. (1987). *The closest of enemies: A personal and diplomatic account of U.S.-Cuban relations since 1957.* New York: Norton.

Symons, M. (1982). *One continuous picnic: A history of eating in Australia.* Adelaide: Duck Press.

Tsing, A. L. (2000). "The global situation." *Cultural Anthropology* 15(3):327–60.

Tsing, A. L. (2005). *Friction: An ethnography of global connection.* Princeton, NJ: Princeton University Press.

United Nations Development Programme. (1996). *Urban agriculture: Food, jobs, sustainable cities.* New York: UNDP.

Vlaum, S. (2001). "Interview with Bill Mollison 2011." Seeds of Change. Retrieved January 2011 from *www.seedsofchange.com/cutting_edge/interview.aspx.*

Warner, S. B., and H. Durlach. (1987). *To dwell is to garden: A history of Boston's community gardens.* Boston: Northeastern University Press.

Wright, J. (2009). *Sustainable agriculture and food security in an era of oil scarcity: Lessons from Cuba.* London: Earthscan.

References

Wright, S., T. Phillips, J. McKenzie, and A. Tiller. (1996). *Urban permaculture in Havana: Implications for sustainable cities of the south and north*. Paper presented at the IPC-VI Conference, Designing for a Sustainable Future, Perth and Bridgetown, Australia, September 27–October 7.

Index

Italicized page numbers denote figures and tables

CPSIA information can be obtained
at www.ICGtesting.com
Printed in the USA
LVHW101729191122
733603LV00002B/151